PENGUIN BOOKS

CHRISTMAS CRACKERS

John Julius Norwich was born in 1929. He was educated at
Upper Canada College, Toronto, at Eton, at the University of
Strasbourg and, after a spell of National Service in the Navy, at
New College, Oxford, where he took a degree in French and
Russian. In 1952 he joined the Foreign Service and remained in
it for twelve years, serving at the Embassies in Belgrade and
Beirut and with the British delegation to the Disarmament
Conference at Geneva. In 1964 he resigned from the service in
order to write.

He has published two books on the medieval Norman Kingdom
in Sicily, *The Normans in the South* and *The Kingdom in the Sun*,
and the two travel-cum-history books, *Mount Athos* (with Reresby
Sitwell) and *Sahara*. The first volume of his history of the Venetian
Republic, *Venice, the Rise to Empire*, was published in 1977, and the
second, *Venice, the Greatness and the Fall*, in 1981. In addition he
writes and presents historical documentaries for BBC television.

Lord Norwich is chairman of the Venice in Peril Fund, a
trustee of the Civic Trust, and a member of the Executive and
Properties Committees of the National Trust. He is also a
member of the Liberal Party in the House of Lords.

He is married to a painter, has two children and lives in Little
Venice, London.

Christmas Crackers

being ten commonplace
selections by

JOHN JULIUS NORWICH

1970 ~ 1979

PENGUIN BOOKS

Penguin Books Ltd, Harmondsworth, Middlesex, England
Penguin Books, 40 West 23rd Street, New York, New York 10010, U.S.A.
Penguin Books Australia Ltd, Ringwood, Victoria, Australia
Penguin Books Canada Ltd, 2801 John Street, Markham, Ontario, Canada L3R 1B4
Penguin Books (N.Z.) Ltd, 182–190 Wairau Road, Auckland 10, New Zealand

First published in one volume by Allen Lane 1980
Reprinted with additional material 1981
Published in Penguin Books 1982
Reprinted 1983

Made and printed in Great Britain
by Richard Clay (The Chaucer Press) Ltd,
Bungay, Suffolk
Set in Monotype Ehrhardt

Look, what thy memory cannot contain
Commit to these waste blanks, and thou shalt find
Those children nursed, deliver'd from thy brain,
To take a new acquaintance of thy mind.

Shakespeare, Sonnet 77

Contents

It must be nearly a quarter of a century since my mother sent me, as a birthday present, a beautiful volume bound in blue Nigerian goatskin, every one of its 150-odd pages completely blank. She had, I think, intended it for use as a diary, or perhaps as a visitors' book for people who came to stay with us in Beirut, where we were then living; but I have never been much of a hand at diaries – except other people's – and by the time it reached me a new crisis had blown up in the Middle East, which meant that for several months we had no visitors at all. Anyway, I had other ideas. A sunset curfew may have its disadvantages, but it affords a marvellous opportunity for catching up with one's reading; and I had recently got into the habit of copying out into a little notebook various passages that had particularly taken my fancy and that, for one reason or another, I wanted to remember. The notebook was fast filling up and, as it did so, becoming increasingly dog-eared; the blue goatskin seemed in every respect a worthier repository for my treasures; and the next few evenings were spent in happy transcription.

Then a strange thing happened. In the splendour of their new environment, the various passages of prose and poetry that I had copied out seemed to take on a new, corporate identity. What had started off simply as a pile of literary odds and ends, to be added to at the whim of the moment, suddenly became a collection, something to be nurtured and cultivated and cared for. And the beautiful volume with its tooled and gilded decoration around the edges and the spine – that too I found myself contemplating with a new pleasure, not untinged with pride. No longer was it just a fine piece of binding; it was my commonplace book.

As the years went by, the blue volume filled up and was succeeded by a similar one in red; and I came to realize that I had stumbled, half accidentally, on one of the most wholly satisfying subjects for collection that the world has to offer. First of all, it costs literally nothing; nicely bound volumes are useful for providing the initial impetus and for creating the sense of pride that every collector must develop to keep him going, but they are in no way essential. Secondly, being totally divorced from monetary wealth, it knows no restrictions of size or scope, only those limitations which the collector himself decides to impose; it follows that no other form of collection can so fully reflect his taste and his personality. Thirdly, he is on his own, far from the world of catalogues and sale-rooms, experts and dealers. Indeed, one of the first lessons he learns is never to go out looking for anything; he is very unlikely to find it if he does, and the very act of searching seems in some curious way to blunt his antennae. If he can only keep them sharp, there is no telling when and where he will make his next trouvaille. He may not even need to wait till he next picks up a book; a chance remark, a letter from a friend, an opera programme, an advertisement, the instruction book for the new washing machine, a visit to a country church, a notice in a hotel room or a railway station, any of these things, or a thousand others, can reveal the unexpected nugget of pure gold.

In one respect, however, the commonplace collector shows himself to be no different from the rest of his kind. Like them he feels, sooner or later, an irrepressible urge to share his collection with others; and it was in response to that urge, ten years ago, that I hit upon the idea of having a little booklet printed containing a couple of dozen of my favourite items, and of distributing it to friends as a sort of glorified Christmas card. Production costs in those days were not excessive and might, I thought, be largely offset if I were to order a few more copies than I needed and persuade one or two friendly booksellers to dispose of them as best they could. The title, as always, posed a bit of a problem. The first one I thought of, A Christmas Cracker, seemed something less than inspired; but nobody seemed able to think of a better one so I settled for it, adding the year – 1970 – just in case the outcome of the experiment made it seem worth repeating at any time in the future.

Rather to my surprise, it worked – and better than I had dared to hope. A fortnight before Christmas my two commercial outlets, Heywood Hill and Vanessa Williams-Ellis, had both sold out and I was down to my last copy. Then an American lady whom I had never met – though she and her husband have now become dear friends – telephoned to ask if she could have fifty more printed at her own expense. I replied that nothing would give me more pleasure, asking only that she should run off an extra dozen for me. There was encouragement indeed; and in the following year I not only prepared a new Cracker but upped the print order, in a reckless burst of optimism, from two hundred to three.

And so the uncertain seedling became a moderately hardy annual, and I now find myself writing an introduction to the combined harvest of the first decade. Nothing has been omitted; there are, however, several additions. One of the most agreeable incidental pleasures of Cracker-production has been the response from readers – friends and strangers alike – who have contributed comments on one item or another, often including further quotations or excerpts which have a direct bearing on the first. Some of these comments and quotations have found their way into the following year's Cracker; others have had to wait till now to see the light of day. I have included them in this book wherever seemed most suitable; otherwise, all items appear in the same order as in the original, if only because I gave a good deal of thought to the matter at the time. In the commonplace books themselves – the leather-bound jobs, I mean – I try to preserve the all-important quality of haphazardness by letting the current volume fall open where it will and copying in the new entry at the first empty page; but in a Cracker of only twenty-four pages altogether that same quality has to be worked for, both in the selection of items and in their final arrangement: the grave must lie down with the gay, the poetry with the prose, the English with the French, the cynical with the sad; and it is not always easy to make them do so.

Contributions have also come in that are unrelated to anything that has appeared before, simply on the strength of their own merits. Many of these, too, have appeared in subsequent Crackers – not all of them, I am ashamed to confess, with proper acknowledgement of their sources. In those instances where the omission was the result of a simple oversight, I have seized the present opportunity to repair it; but I have a nasty feeling that there were a number of others where, in my excitement at the gift, I somehow forgot to record the name of the giver. To these still unacknowledged benefactors I can only apologize, assuring them that my apparent ingratitude is due to sheer absent-mindedness and not through any wish to pass off their serendipity as my own.

Finally, a word to those who have sent me items which I have not used. Once again, I implore them not to think me ungrateful, still less to assume that, because their contribution does not appear in the very next Cracker, it has been permanently rejected. There is, I find, a widely held misconception that each year's edition is made up of items culled in the course of the previous twelve months. In fact, it is simply a selection made, usually in the course of a single summer Sunday afternoon, from the four completed commonplace books – the blue and the red having more recently been joined by a brown and a green – already on my shelf. This means that while a few pieces in any given Cracker may well be recent additions to the hoard, others may have been waiting twenty years or more for publication. The mix is everything; it imposes its own rules, and will not be hurried.

None the less, there is plenty of splendid material which, though I have enthusiastically transcribed it into the books, will probably never take its place in a Cracker. Much of it is of my own finding; for the rest, I can offer no explanation, except to say that, just as a novelist or playwright sometimes sees his characters assuming individual personalities that he had never intended for them, so the Crackers, in their modest way, also seem to have developed, over ten years, their own interior logic. Some items fit; others, of equally high quality and every bit as welcome, somehow refuse to settle down. When that happens, I hope that their kind sponsors will understand, and not be discouraged from sending further contributions.

For this book is only a milestone; it is not the end of the road. Soon after it is published, the 1980 Cracker will be on sale at the two bookshops mentioned above, and at Hatchards and John Sandoe, who have since joined them as regular purveyors. (If any other bookseller would care to chance his arm on a few copies, he has only to let me know.) How many more editions will follow is anybody's guess; I should like to keep it up as long as I can, if only because I personally enjoy it so much – far more, I feel quite certain, than anybody else.

Apart from those who have sent contributions, used and unused, I should also like to record my very special thanks to Mrs Alison Henning, without whose encouragement – already described – the first Cracker might easily have been the last; to John Saumarez Smith of Heywood Hill, whose enthusiasm – to say nothing of his salesmanship – has been an annual tonic; to

Vanessa Williams-Ellis, equally faithful from the start of it all; to my secretary Jean Curtis, who has tackled all the typing – agonizingly complicated as in some of the entries, or paralytically boring as in the several hundred envelopes required every year – with equal cheerfulness, as well as attending to the business side; and to all those, known and unknown, who have bought copies year by year and kept this whole slightly dotty enterprise going as long as it has.

JOHN JULIUS NORWICH

Cap Haitien, December 1979

Postscript, 1981

The first appearance of this book met with a success unexpected by author and publisher alike, with the result that supplies quickly became exhausted. It did, however, evoke a few valuable contributions immediately relevant to certain of the entries, which its reprinting a year later has given me the opportunity to include.

I am also glad to report that in 1981 the annual Cracker *will be on sale for the first time in both Oxford and Cambridge – at Robin Waterfield's and Heffer's respectively.*

J.J.N.

A Christmas Cracker

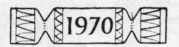

1970

A ledger-slab in the church of Bramfield, Suffolk, reads:

Between the Remains of her Brother EDWARD
And of her Husband ARTHUR
Here lies the Body of BRIDGETT APPLEWHAITE
Once BRIDGETT NELSON.
After the Fatigues of a Married Life,
Born by her with Incredible Patience,
For four years and three Quarters, bating three Weeks,
And after the Enjoiment of the Glorious Freedom
Of an Early and Unblemisht Widowhood,
For four Years and Upwards,
She Resolved to run the Risk of a Second Marriage-Bed
But DEATH forbad the Banns –
And having with an Apoplectick Dart
(The same Instrument, with which he had Formerly
Dispatch't her Mother),
Touch't the most Vital part of her Brain;
She must have fallen Directly to the Ground,
(as one Thunder-strook)
If she had not been Catch't and Supported
by her Intended Husband.
Of which Invisible Bruise,
After a Struggle, for above Sixty Hours
With that Grand Enemy to Life,
(But the Certain and Mercifull Friend to Helpless Old Age,)
In Terrible Convulsions, Plaintive Groans, or Stupefying Sleep,
Without recovery of her Speech, or Senses,
She Dyed, on the 12th Day of Sept: in ye Year
of our Lord, 1737
and
of her own age, 44.

Behold! I come as a Thief. Rev. 16th Chr., 15th v.

About mid-Lent, the King with his sonne and the legat came to London, where at Westminster a conuocation of the cleargie was called, but when the legat was set, and the archbishop of Canturburie on his right hand as primat of the realme, the archbishop of Yorke comming in, and disdaining to sit on the left, where he might séeme to giue preheminence unto the archbishop of Canturburie (vnmanerlie inough indeed) swasht him downe, meaning to thrust himselfe in betwixt the legat, and the archbishop of Canturburie. And when belike the said archbishop of Canturburie was loth to remooue, he set his buttocks inst in his lap, but he scarslie touched the archbishops skirt with his bum, when the bishops and other chapleins with their seruants stept to him, pulled him away, and threw him to the ground, and beginning to lay on him with bats and fists, the archbishop of Canturburie yeelding good for euill, sought to saue him from their hands. Thus was verified in him that sage sentence,

Nunquam periculum sine periculo vincitur.

The archbishop of Yorke with his rent rochet got up, and awaie he went to the king with a great complaint against the archbishop of Canturburie: but when vpon examination of the matter the truth was knowne, he was well laught at for his labour, and that was all the remedie he got.

There is no spectacle more agreeable than to observe an old friend fall from a roof-top.

Confucius

The same point occurred to Lucretius, more or less:

> Suave, mari magno turbantibus aequora ventis,
> E terra magnum alterius spectare laborem.

> (How pleasant to gaze out to sea, when the waves are lashed by the tempest,
> And watch, from the safety of land, the desperate struggles of others).

And to La Rochefoucauld, though perhaps he put it a little more tactfully:

> Dans l'adversité de nos meilleurs amis nous trouvons
> quelque chose, qui ne nous déplaist pas.

Or, as Swift gleefully translated it:

> In all distresses of our friends
> We first consult our private ends,
> While nature, kindly bent to ease us,
> Points out some circumstance to please us.

I like Confucius best.

Went down to the Bath Flower Show in Sydney College Gardens. Found the first train going down was an Excursion train and took a ticket for it. The carriage was nearly full. In the Box tunnel as there was no lamp, the people began to strike foul brimstone matches and hand them to each other all down the carriage. All the time we were in the tunnel these lighted matches were travelling from hand to hand in the darkness. Each match lasted the length of the carriage and the red ember was thrown out of the opposite window, by which time another lighted match was seen travelling down the carriage. The carriage was chock full of brimstone fumes, the windows both nearly shut, and by the time we got out of the tunnel I was almost suffocated. Then a gentleman tore a lady's pocket handkerchief in two, seized one fragment, blew his nose with it, and put the rag in his pocket. She then seized his hat from his head, while another lady said that the dogs of Wootton Bassett were much more sociable than the people.

From the diary of the Rev. Francis Kilvert,
Wednesday, 18 May 1870

On Thursday, 21 July, he writes:

The Vicar of St Ives says the smell of fish there is sometimes so terrific as to stop the church clock.

Some dictionary definitions:

BAFFONA, *f.* Woman with not unpleasing moustache.

> Hoare's *Short Italian Dictionary,*
> Cambridge, 1954

CARPHOLOGY. Delirious fumbling with the bedclothes, &c.

> *Concise Oxford Dictionary*

DOTTEREL. A species of plover (*Eudromias morinellus*): said to be so simple that it readily allows itself to be taken.
1. This dotrell is a lytell fonde byrde, for it helpeth in maner to take it selfe 1526.

> *Oxford Dictionary*

NATURA ... 6. the female pudenda; 7. the male organ of generation; 8. God.

> *Italian Dictionary* by Davenport and Comelati,
> London, 1873

Here is a letter written by a sailor on H.M.S. Royal Sovereign *immediately after the battle of Trafalgar:*

Honoured Fathre,
This comes to tell you that I am alive and hearty except three fingers; but that's not much, it might have been my head. I told brother Tom I should like to see a greadly battle, and I have seen one, and we have peppered the Combined rarely (off Trafalgar); and for the matter of that, they fought us pretty tightish for French and Spanish. Three of our mess are killed, and four more of us winged. But to tell you the truth of it, when the game began, I wished myself at Warnborough with my plough again; but when they had given us one duster, and I found myself snug and tight, I set to in good earnest, and thought no more about being killed than if I were at Murrell Green Fair, and I was presently as busy and as black as a collier. How my fingers got knocked overboard I don't know, but off they are, and I never missed them till I wanted them. You see, by my writing, it was my left hand, so I can write to you and fight for my King yet. We have taken a rare parcel of ships, but the wind is so rough we cannot bring them home, else I should roll in money, so we are busy smashing 'em, and blowing 'em up wholesale.

Our dear Admiral Nelson is killed! so we have paid pretty sharply for licking 'em. I never set eyes on him, for which I am both sorry and glad; for to be sure, I should like to have seen him – but then, all the men in our ship are such soft toads, they have done nothing but blast their eyes, and cry, ever since he was killed. God bless you! chaps that fought like the devil, sit down and cry like a wench. I am still in the *Royal Sovereign*, but the Admiral [Collingwood] has left her, for she is like a horse without a bridle, so he is in a frigate that he may be here and there and everywhere, for he's as *cute* as here and there one, and as bold as a lion, for all he can cry! I saw his tears with my own eyes, when the boat hailed and said my Lord was dead. So no more at present from

Your dutiful Son,
Sam

Quel que soit le souci que ta jeunesse endure,
Laisse-la s'élargir, cette sainte blessure
Que les noirs séraphins t'ont faite au fond du cœur;
Rien ne nous rend si grands qu'une grande douleur.

Alfred de Musset

Admirable advice to travellers from Baedeker's Handbook to Palestine and Syria, with the Chief Routes through Mesopotamia and Babylonia, *1906*:

INTERCOURSE WITH ORIENTALS

Most Orientals regard the European traveller as a Croesus, and sometimes as a madman, so unintelligible to them are the objects and pleasures of travelling. They therefore demand Bakhshîsh almost as a right from those who seem so much better supplied with this world's goods. He who gives is a good man. . . . The custom of scattering small coins for the sake of the amusement furnished by the consequent scramble is an insult to poverty that no rightminded traveller will offer.

Beneath the interminable protestations of friendship with which the traveller is overwhelmed lurks in most cases the demon of cupidity. . . . It will be impossible to avoid extortions or overcharges altogether, and it is better to reconcile oneself to this than to poison one's enjoyment by too much suspicion.

MONEY

English and French gold (as also Russian) passes everywhere; German gold can be changed without loss only at some German houses. Foreign silver is prohibited all over Turkey, but francs and shillings are taken at the sea-ports, and in Jerusalem and Damascus; marks are generally refused. Egyptian money is refused everywhere.

Annette had never been in love, although she was not without experience. She had been deflowered at seventeen by a friend of her brother on the suggestion of the latter. Nicholas would have arranged it when she was sixteen, only he needed her just then for a black mass.

Iris Murdoch,
The Flight from the Enchanter

There is something curiously refreshing about really bad poems, particularly by really good poets. Wordsworth's sonnet endearingly entitled 'To the Spade of a Friend' can boast what must be one of the most atrocious opening lines ever written:

Spade! With which Wilkinson hath tilled his lands ...

Another, addressed to one of the leading abolitionists of the slave trade, runs it close:

Clarkson! It was an obstinate hill to climb:
How toilsome – nay, how dire – it was, by thee
Is known; by none perhaps so feelingly.

Here is Richard Crashaw on the weeping Magdalen:

And now where'er He strays,
Among the Galilean mountains,
Or more unwelcome ways,
He's followed by two faithful fountains;
Two walking baths; two weeping motions;
Portable and compendious oceans ...

And even Shakespeare could nod. Take, for example, the following verse from Venus and Adonis:

'Nay then' quoth Adon, 'you will fall again
Into your idle overhandled theme;
The kiss I gave you is bestowed in vain,
And all in vain you strive against the stream;
   For, by this black-fac'd night, desire's foul nurse,
   Your treatise makes me like you worse and worse.'

The lowest trees have topps, the ante her gall,
The flie her spleen, the little sparke his heat;
The slender hears cast shadows, though but small,
And bees have stinges, although they be not great;
   Seas have their sourse, and soe have shallow springes:
   And Love is Love, in beggers and in Kinges.

Wher waters smothest ronne, ther deepest are the foords,
The diall stirs, yet none perceives it moove;
The firmest fayth is fownd in fewest woordes,
The turtles doe not singe, and yet they love;
   True heartes have ears and eyes, no tongues to speake:
   They heare and see, and sigh, and then they breake.

Sir Edward Dyer (c. 1545–1607)

Sir Edward Dyer was not the only poet in his family. Colmworth church in Bedfordshire contains a lovely monument erected in 1641 by Lady Catherine to her husband, Sir William ; I feel sure she wrote this verse herself:

My dearest dust, could not thy hasty day
Afford thy drowszy patience leave to stay
One hower longer: so that we might either
Sate up, or gone to bedd together?
But since thy finisht labour hath possest
Thy weary limbs with early rest,
Enjoy it sweetly: and thy widdowe bride
Shall soone repose her by thy slumbring side.
Whose business, now, is only to prepare
My nightly dress, and call to prayre:
Mine eyes wax heavy and ye day growes old.
The dew falls thick, my belovd growes cold.
Draw, draw ye closed curtaynes: and make roome:
My dear, my dearest dust; I come, I come.

In 1967 we awarded the Duff Cooper Memorial Prize to a book called The Peregrine. *Its author, J. A. Baker, had never written a book before. I didn't think anyone could really interest me in bird-watching; but he can, because he can write like this:*

The first bird I searched for was the nightjar, which used to nest in the valley. Its song is like the sound of a stream of wine spilling from a height into a deep and booming cask. It is an odorous sound, with a bouquet that rises to the quiet sky. In the glare of day it would seem thinner and drier, but dusk mellows it and gives it vintage. If a song could smell, this song would smell of crushed grapes and almonds and dark wood. The sound spills out, and none of it is lost. The whole wood brims with it. Then it stops. Suddenly, unexpectedly. But the ear hears it still, a prolonged and fading echo, draining and winding out among the surrounding trees.

I'm very fond of palindromes. Perhaps my favourite of them all is :

Live dirt up a side-track carted is a putrid evil.

J. A. Lindon must be credited with two gems :

Straw? No, too stupid a fad. I put *soot* on warts.

and – perhaps the only one of reasonable length that might pass unnoticed in any twentieth-century novel :

'Norma is as selfless as I am, Ron.'

But the palm for the longest goes to W.H. Auden :

T. Eliot, top bard, notes putrid tang emanating, is sad. I'd assign it a name: 'Gnat dirt upset on drab pot toilet.'

And while we're at it, there are even a couple of classical ones to be quoted. First, the lament of the Roman moths :

In girum imus noctes, et consumimur igni.

And finally the inscription engraved on the phiale in St Sophia :

Νίψον ἀνόμημα, μὴ μόναν ὄψιν.
(Wash not only my face, but also my transgressions.)

Under the willow the willow
  I heard the butcher-bird sing,
Come out you fine young fellow
  From under your mother's wing.
I'll show you the magic garden
  That hangs in the beamy air,
The way of the lynx and the angry Sphinx
  And the fun of the freezing fair.

Lie down lie down with my daughter
  Beneath the Arabian tree,
Gaze on your face in the water
  Forget the scribbling sea.
Your pillow the nine bright shiners,
  Your bed the spilling sand,
But the terrible toy of my lily-white boy
  Is the gun in his innocent hand.

You must take off your clothes for the doctor,
  And stand as straight as a pin,
His hand of stone on your white breast-bone
  Where the bullets all go in.
They'll dress you in lawn and linen
  And fill you with Plymouth gin,
  O the devil may wear a rose in his hair
  I'll wear my fine doe-skin.

My mother weeps as I leave her
  But I tell her it won't be long,
The murderers wail in Wandsworth Gaol
  But I shoot a more popular song.
Down in the enemy country
  Under the enemy tree
There lies a lad whose heart has gone bad
  Waiting for me, for me.

He says I have no culture
  And that when I've stormed the pass
I shall fall on the farm with a smoking arm
  And ravish his bonny lass.
Under the willow the willow
  Death spreads her dripping wings
And caught in the snare of the bleeding air
  The butcher-bird sings, sings, sings.

Charles Causley

Pleasant to me is the glittering of the sun upon these margins, because it flickers so.

Marginal note by an Irish scribe
in a ninth-century manuscript

... These vital interests should render Great Britain the earnest and unyielding opponent of the Russian projects of annexation and aggrandisement. . . . Having come thus far on the way to universal empire is it probable that this gigantic, swollen power will pause in its career? With the Albanian coast . . . she is in the very centre of the Adriatic. . . . It would appear that the natural frontier of Russia runs from Danzig or perhaps Stettin to Trieste. And as sure as conquest follows conquest and annexation follows annexation, so surely would the conquest of Turkey by Russia be only the prelude to the annexation of Hungary, Prussia, Galicia and the ultimate realization of the Slavonic Empire. The arrest of the Russian scheme of annexation is a matter of the highest moment. In this instance the interests of democracy and of England go hand in hand.

From the *New York Tribune*, 12 April 1853,
by its European correspondent, Karl Marx

Johnson, I believe, did not play at draughts after leaving College, by which he suffered; for it would have afforded him an innocent soothing relief from the melancholy which distressed him so often. . . . The game of draughts we know is peculiarly calculated to fix the attention without straining it. There is a composure and gravity in draughts which insensibly tranquillises the mind; and, accordingly, the Dutch are fond of it.

Boswell, *The Life of Johnson*

Chess, on the other hand, is headier stuff – at least according to Robert Burton. In The Anatomy of Melancholy *he writes:*

Chesse-play is a good and witty exercise of the mind, for some kind of men, and fit for such melancholy (Rhasis holds) as are idle, and have extravagant impertinent thoughts, or troubled with cares; nothing better to distract their mind, and alter their meditations; invented (some say) by the generall of an army in a famine, to keep souldiers from mutiny: but if it proceed from over much study, in such a case it may do more harm than good; it is a game too troublesome for some mens braines, too full of anxiety, all out as bad as study; besides, it is a testy cholerick game, and very offensive to him that loseth the mate. William the Conqueror, in his younger yeares playing at chesse with the prince of France (Dauphine was not annexed to that crown in those dayes) losing a mate, knocked the chesse-board about his pate, which was a cause afterward of much enmity betwixt them.

Here is Paddy Leigh-Fermor in Antigua :

At the end of this broad street, which sloped slightly as it receded from the shallow harbour, an Anglican but extremely baroque-looking cathedral stood among the trees. The twin towers that flanked the classical façade were topped by polygonal bronze cupolas and everything in the treatment of the massive stone fabric led one to believe that it had been built in the late seventeenth or the eighteenth century. Accustomed as we were becoming to surprises of this kind, we were taken aback by the information that it was built – on the exact lines, though, of its predecessor, which an earthquake had destroyed – in 1847. There was nothing inside to impair the illusion. The spacious and airy proportions, the Corinthian pillars, the panelling, the gilding, and the lettering of the Ten Commandments all belonged to the Augustan Age of English architecture. And the presiding Godhead, one felt (as one feels in all the churches built between Wren and the Gothic revival) is also a denizen of that prolonged and opulent afternoon. He is not the mysterious Presence of the Middle Ages, nor is He the avenging Thunderer of the Puritans, nor the top-hatted Puseyite of later times, nor yet the stoled and white-overalled Scientist of today. Gazing through the thin, drained atmosphere at the fluted columns and the acanthus leaves, the cornucopias and the formal flutter of the ribbons of wood that secure the carved festoons, our island Deity of the reigns of Queen Anne and the Georges slowly begins, like an emerging portrait by Kneller or Gainsborough or Raeburn, to take shape. The placid features assemble and the misty grey eyes with their compound expression of humour and severity; the heavy judicial curls of the wig, the amaranthine volume of the robes, and the soft blue of the Garter are unfolded in mid-air. A forefinger marks the place in a pocket edition of Voltaire; on a marble table, the tea-time sunlight rests on the vellum-bound Pentateuch and the Odes of Horace, and gently glows on the scales, the marshal's baton and the metal strawberry-leaves. A heavy curtain is looped back, and beyond, with the sweep of soft shadow and faded gold of a gentleman's deer-park, lie the mild prospects of Paradise, the pillared rotunda reflected in the lake, the dreaming swans, and at last, the celestial mansion built by Vanburgh, rearing, against the sky of Sèvres blue and the whipped-cream clouds, its colonnaded entablature, its marble Graces and its urns. . . . This Elysian fancy paled all at once at the sight, on the cushion of one of the pews in the chancel, of the black pom-pom of a biretta. The Hanoverian vision grew vaporous and confused with anachronistic draughts from Oxford and Rome; and vanished.

The Traveller's Tree

Weep no more, woful shepherds, weep no more,
For Lycidas your sorrow is not dead.
Sunk though he be beneath the watry floar,
So sinks the day-star in the Ocean bed,
And yet anon repairs his drooping head,
And tricks his beams, and with new spangled Ore,
Flames in the forehead of the morning sky.

Milton, *Lycidas*

That marvellous last line is echoed, curiously enough, by Victor Hugo in Mazeppa. *This is how he describes the artist carried away by his genius:*

Il traverse d'un vol, sur tes ailes de flamme,
Tous les champs du possible et les mondes de l'âme,
   Boit au fleuve éternel,
Dans la nuit orageuse ou la nuit étoilée,
Sa chevelure, aux crins des comètes mêlée,
   Flamboie au front du ciel . . .

Milton has another superb astronomical metaphor in Book I of Paradise Lost:
                     As when the Sun new ris'n
Looks through the Horizontal misty air
Shorn of his Beams, or from behind the Moon
In dim Eclips disastrous twilight sheds
On half the Nations, and with fear of change
Perplexes monarchs.

One of the most unusual coronations in history must have been that of the
Persian King Shapur II in A.D. *309. Here is Gibbon on the subject :*

The wife of Hormouz remained pregnant at the time of her
husband's death, and the uncertainty of the sex, as well as of the
event, excited the ambitious hopes of the princes of the house of
Sassan. The apprehensions of civil war were at length removed by
the positive assurance of the Magi that the widow of Hormouz had
conceived, and would safely produce a son. Obedient to the voice of
superstition, the Persians prepared, without delay, the ceremony of
his coronation. A royal bed, on which the queen lay in state, was
exhibited in the midst of the palace; the diadem was placed on the
spot which might be supposed to conceal the future heir of
Artaxerxes, and the prostrate satraps adored the majesty of their
invisible and insensible sovereign.

My mother taught me to read with the aid of a splendid little volume called Reading Without Tears, or a Pleasant Mode of Learning to Read, *by the Author of 'Peep of Day', &c. It was published in 1861 and deserves reprinting. Where I was concerned, it did its job swiftly and, as promised, painlessly ; but the other day I looked through it again, and wondered. Here are two extracts :*

What is the mat-ter with that lit-tle boy?

He has ta-ken poi-son. He saw a cup of poi-son on the shelf. He said 'This seems sweet stuff.' So he drank it.

Why did he take it with-out leave?

Can the doc-tor cure him? Will the poi-son des-troy him? He must die. The poi-son has des-troyed him.

Wil-li-am climb-ed up-stairs to the top of the house, and went to the gun-pow-der clos-et. He fil-led the can-is-ter. Why did he not go down-stairs quickly? It came into his fool-ish mind, 'I will go in-to the nur-se-ry and fright-en my lit-tle bro-thers and sis-ters.'

It was his de-light to fright-en the chil-dren. How un-kind! He found them a-lone with-out a nurse. So he was a-ble to play tricks. He throws a lit-tle gun-pow-der in-to the fire. And what hap-pens? The flames dart out and catch the pow-der in the can-is-ter. It is blown up with a loud noise. The chil-dren are thrown down, they are in flames. The win-dows are bro-ken. The house is sha-ken.

Mis-ter Mor-ley rush-es up-stairs. What a sight! All his chil-dren ly-ing on the floor burn-ing. The ser-vants help to quench the flames. They go for a cab to take the chil-dren to the hos-pit-al. The doc-tor says, 'The chil-dren are blind, they will soon die.'

Charles, Duke of Orleans, was the father of Louis XII of France. He was taken prisoner by the English at Agincourt, and held to ransom in England for over a quarter of a century, during the best years of his life. But that did not prevent him from writing the happiest poem I know.

Le temps a laissié son manteau
De vent, de froidure et de pluye,
Et s'est vestu de brouderie,
De soleil luyant, cler et beau.
Il n'y a beste, ne oyseau
Qu'en son jargon ne chant ou crie:
Le temps a laissié son manteau
De vent, de froidure et de pluye.
Rivière, fontaine et ruisseau
Portent, en livrée jolie,
Gouttes d'argent d'orfaverie,
Chascun s'abille de nouveau.
Le temps a laissié son manteau.

A
Christmas
Cracker

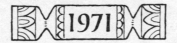

JOHN COLET, D.D., Deane of St Paule's, London. After the Conflagration (his Monument being broken) somebody made a little hole towards the upper edge of his Coffin, which was closed like the coffin of a Pye and was full of a Liquour which conserved the body. Mr Wyld and Ralph Greatorex tasted it and 'twas of a kind of insipid tast, something of an Ironish tast. The Coffin was of Lead, and layd in the Wall about 2 foot ½ above the surface of the Floore.

This was a strange rare way of conserving a Corps: perhaps it was a Pickle, as for Beefe, whose Saltness in so many years the Lead might sweeten and render insipid. The body felt, to the probe of a stick which they thrust into a chinke, like boyld Brawne.

John Aubrey

On se demande, devant certains livres: qui peut les lire? – devant certains gens: que peuvent-ils lire?... puis ça finit par s'accrocher.

Les poissons meurent le ventre en l'air et remontent à la surface; c'est leur façon de tomber.

Gide, Journal

John Guest has pointed out an interesting parallel to this second thought – Andrew Young's poem 'A Dead Mole':

Strong-shouldered mole,
That so much lived below the ground,
Dug, fought and loved, hunted and fed,
For you to raise a mound
Was as for us to make a hole;
What wonder now that being dead
Your body lies here, stout and square
Buried within the blue vault of the air?

'Ah,' said Mr Woodhouse, shaking his head, and fixing his eye on her with tender concern. The ejaculation in Emma's ear expressed, 'Ah, there is no end of the sad consequences of your going to Southend. It does not bear talking of.' And for a little while she hoped he would not talk of it, and that a silent rumination might suffice to restore him to the relish of his own smooth gruel. After an interval of some minutes, however, he began with:

'I shall always be very sorry that you went to the sea this autumn, instead of coming here.'

'But why should you be sorry, sir? I assure you it did the children a great deal of good.'

'And, moreover, if you must go to the sea, it had better not to have been to Southend. Southend is an unhealthy place. Perry was surprised to hear you had fixed upon Southend.'

'I know there is such an idea with many people, but indeed it is quite a mistake, sir. We all had our health perfectly well there, never found the least inconvenience from the mud, and Mr Wingfield says it is entirely a mistake to suppose the place unhealthy; and I am sure he may be depended on, for he thoroughly understands the nature of the air, and his own brother and family have been there repeatedly.'

'You should have gone to Cromer, my dear, if you went anywhere. Perry was a week at Cromer once, and he holds it to be the best of all the sea bathing places. A fine open sea, he says, and very pure air. And, by what I understand, you might have had lodgings there quite away from the sea – a quarter of a mile off – very comfortable. You should have consulted Perry.'

'But, my dear sir, the difference of the journey; only consider how great it would have been. A hundred miles, perhaps, instead of forty.'

'Ah, my dear, as Perry says, where health is at stake nothing else should be considered, and if one is to travel, there is not much to choose between forty miles and a hundred. Better not move at all, better stay in London altogether, than travel forty miles to get into worse air. This is just what Perry said. It seemed to him a very ill-judged measure.'

Jane Austen, Emma, Ch. 12

Two passages from Troilus and Cressida :

Injurious time now with a robber's haste
Crams his rich thievery up, he knows not how:
As many farewells as be stars in heaven,
With distinct breath, and consign'd kisses to them,
He fumbles up into a loose adieu,
And scants us with a single famished kiss,
Distasted with the salt of broken tears.

He brought a Grecian queen, whose youth and freshness
Wrinkles Apollo's, and makes pale the morning.

Sonntag waren wir in Pompeji. – Es ist viel Unheil in der Welt geschehen, aber wenig das den Nachkommen so viel Freude gemacht hätte.

(On Sunday we were in Pompeii. There have been many disasters in this world, but few which have given so much delight to posterity.)

Goethe, Italian Journey

This is one of the relatively few opinions expressed by Goethe in the diary of his travels through Italy and Sicily with which most of us could agree. On almost every page one is staggered by the difference between his reactions and what one's own would have been. He passed through Assisi, for example, without bothering to look inside either of the two churches. And the following incident, which occurred during his stay in Palermo, shows still more forcibly the gulf separating his century from ours. (The translation is by W. H. Auden and Elizabeth Mayer.)

The fair spring weather and the luxuriant vegetation lent an air of grace and peace to the whole valley, which our stupid guide proceeded to ruin with his erudition, for he started telling us in great detail how, long ago, Hannibal had given battle here and what stupendous feats of valour had taken place on this very spot. I angrily rebuked him for such an odious evocation of defunct ghosts. It was bad enough, I said, that from time to time crops have to be trampled down, if not always by elephants, still by horses and men, but at least one need not shock the imagination out of its peaceful dreams by recalling scenes of savage violence from the past.

Goethe, clearly, had no time for 'vibrations' – unlike, for example, John Keats, who wrote in Endymion:

Then old songs waken from unclouded tombs;
Old ditties sigh above their father's grave;
Ghosts of melodious prophesyings rave
Round every spot where trod Apollo's foot;
Bronze clarions awake, and faintly bruit
Where long ago a giant battle was;
And from the turf a lullaby doth pass
In every place where infant Orpheus slept.

The sister of Valentinian was educated in the palace of Ravenna, and as her marriage might be productive of some danger to the state, she was raised, by the title of *Augusta**, above the hopes of the most presumptuous subject. But the fair Honoria had no sooner attained the sixteenth year of her age than she detested the importunate greatness which must for ever exclude her from the comforts of honourable love; in the midst of vain and unsatisfactory pomp Honoria sighed, yielded to the impulse of nature, and threw herself into the arms of her chamberlain Eugenius. Her guilt and shame (such is the absurd language of imperious man) were soon betrayed by the appearances of pregnancy: but the disgrace of the royal family was published to the world by the imprudence of the Empress Placidia, who dismissed her daughter, after a strict and shameful confinement, to a remote exile at Constantinople. The unhappy princess passed twelve or fourteen years in the irksome society of the sisters of Theodosius and their chosen virgins, to whose *crown* Honoria could no longer aspire, and whose monastic assiduity of prayer, fasting and vigils she reluctantly imitated. Her impatience of long and hopeless celibacy urged her to embrace a strange and desperate resolution. The name of Attila was familiar and formidable at Constantinople, and his frequent embassies entertained a perpetual intercourse between his camp and the imperial palace. In the pursuit of love, or rather of revenge, the daughter of Placidia sacrificed every duty and every prejudice, and offered to deliver her person into the arms of a barbarian of whose language she was ignorant, whose figure was scarcely human, and whose religion and manners she abhorred. By the ministry of a faithful eunuch she transmitted to Attila a ring, the pledge of her affection, and earnestly conjured him to claim her as a lawful spouse to whom he had been secretly betrothed. These indecent advances were received, however, with coldness and disdain; and the king of the Huns continued to multiply the number of his wives till his love was awakened by the more forcible passions of ambition and avarice.

* *A medal is still extant which exhibits the pleasing countenance of Honoria, with the title of Augusta ; and on the reverse, the improper legend of* Salus Reipublicae *round the monogram of Christ.*

Gibbon, *The Decline and Fall of the Roman Empire*, Ch. 35

Now must I look as sober and demure as a whore at a Christening.

Capt. Plume,
in *The Recruiting Officer*,
by George Farquhar

An untumultuous fringe of silver foam.

Keats

*This line seems to me every bit as magical as the passage that everybody knows
from the 'Ode to a Nightingale':*

The same that oft-times hath
Charmed magic casements, opening on the foam
Of perilous seas and faery lands forlorn.

*Keats seems to have loved – rightly – the idea of windows looking out over
the water. In 1819 he wrote to his sister Fanny:*

I should like the window to open onto the Lake of Geneva – and
there I'd sit and read all day like the picture of somebody reading.

Another lovely line about water comes in the sonnet 'To Homer':

To visit dolphin-coral in deep seas.

*Apart from this line, the sonnet is rather disappointing – certainly not in the
same league as the one which Chapman's translation had inspired in him two
years before, when he was just twenty-one. It does, however, contain what
Rossetti considered to be 'the greatest line in Keats':*

There is a budding morrow in midnight.

Keats may have been right; but I can't think Rossetti was.

While we are on the subject of Homer and the sea:

> A man who has not read Homer is like a man who has not seen the ocean. There is a great object of which he has no idea.
>
> Bagehot

Which in turn calls to mind the marvellous last words of Sir Isaac Newton:

> I don't know what I may seem to the world. But as to myself I seem to have been only like a boy playing on the seashore and diverting myself in now and then finding a smoother pebble or prettier shell than ordinary, whilst the great ocean of truth lay all undiscovered before me.

I wonder whether Wordsworth had that in mind when he wrote those lines on a bust of Newton:

> The marble index of a mind for ever
> Voyaging through strange seas of thought – alone.

In the late Maurice Bowra's Memories, *he records a letter written to Penelope Betjeman by the Vicar of Baulking:*

Baulking Vicarage

My dear Penelope,

I have been thinking over the question of the playing of the harmonium on Sunday evenings here and have reached the conclusion that I must now take it over myself.

I am very grateful to you for doing it for so long and hate to have to ask you to give it up, but, to put it plainly, your playing has got worse and worse and the disaccord between the harmonium and the congregation is becoming destructive of devotion. People are not very sensitive here, but even some of them have begun to complain, and they are not usually given to doing that. I do not like writing this, but I think you will understand that it is my business to see that divine worship is as perfect as it can be made. Perhaps the crankiness of the instrument has something to do with the trouble. I think it does require a careful and experienced player to deal with it.

Thank you ever so much for stepping so generously into the breach when Sibyl was ill; it was the greatest possible help to me and your results were noticeably better then than now.

Yours ever,
F. P. Harton

This epitaph, by Housman, is inscribed on a plaque in the British War Cemetery on the island of Vis in the Adriatic:

Here dead we lie, because we did not choose
To live and shame the land from which we sprung;
Life, to be sure, is nothing much to lose,
But young men think it is, and we were young.

If I must die,
I will encounter darkness like a bride
And hug it in mine arms.

Measure for Measure

Here are two extracts from the wine catalogues of Mr Gerald Asher, dated 1967 and 1968 respectively:

NUITS-ST GEORGES

Deep colour and big shaggy nose. Rather a jumbly, untidy sort of wine, with fruitiness shooting off one way, firmness another and body pushing about underneath. It will be as comfortable and as comforting as the 1961 Nuits-St Georges once it has pulled its ends in and settled down.

CHÂTEAU LYNCH-BAGES, Grand Crû Classé Pauillac, Château-Bottled

Just the wine for those who like the smell of Verdi. Dark colour, swashbuckling bouquet and ripe flavour. Ready for drinking, but will hold well showing a gradual shift in style as it ages into graceful discretion.

Il est de parfums frais comme des chairs d'enfants,
Doux comme des hautbois, verts comme les prairies,
– Et d'autres corrompus, riches, et triomphants.

Baudelaire

The first ballade I ever knew – though I didn't know it was a ballade – was written by E. C. Bentley at Aalesund in Norway in 1911, after one hates to think what hideous experience. It is called 'A Ballade of Souls'.

The soul of Dante was a white-hot spear;
    The soul of Bonaparte, a thunder-stroke;
The soul of Bismarck was a cask of beer;
    The soul of Blake was roaring fire and smoke;
    The soul of Villon was a tattered cloak;
The soul of Washington, a perfect square;
    The soul of Robespierre, a piece of coke;
But Norway has a soul of sheer despair.

The soul of Dizzy was a chandelier;
    The soul of Shakespeare was a greening oak;
And Swift's, a lordly ship that wouldn't steer;
    Carlyle's, a raven of stentorian croak;
    And Chatterton's, a furnace none would stoke;
The soul of Nietzsche was a rotten pear;
    And bluff King Hal's, a reek to make one choke;
But Norway has a soul of sheer despair.

The soul of Goethe was an opal sphere;
    The soul of Chaucer was a chime that woke
The heart of England; Heine's was a tear;
    And Chatham's was a mighty voice – that broke;
    The soul of Calvin, that lugubrious bloke,
Was principally made of heated air;
    The soul of Herbert Spencer was a joke;
But Norway has a soul of sheer despair.

ENVOI

Prince! Royal Haakon! (Did you know I spoke
    Norwegian?) *Er de syg af det? Jeg er.*
YOU may be happy – though I doubt it, Haak;
    But Norway has a soul of sheer despair.

Riots are the language of the unheard.

Such was the opinion of Dr Martin Luther King. Dr Thomas Arnold, on the other hand, took a different view. His son Matthew, in the first edition (only) of Culture and Anarchy, *quotes him as saying:*

As for rioting, the old Roman way of dealing with *that* is always the right one; flog the rank and file, and fling the ring-leaders from the Tarpeian rock!

Maurice Baring thought that the two novels with the best opening sentences were Don Quixote :

In a village of La Mancha, the name of which I purposely omit, there lived, not long ago, one of those gentlemen who usually keep a lance upon a rack, an old target, a lean horse, and a greyhound for coursing.

and Anna Karenina :

All happy families resemble one another; every unhappy family is unhappy in its own way.

I think I might give the palm to Our Mutual Friend :

In these times of ours, though concerning the exact year there is no need to be precise, a boat of dirty and disreputable appearance, with two figures in it, floated on the Thames, between Southwark Bridge which is of iron, and London Bridge which is of stone, as an autumn evening was closing in.

As for endings, it is surely hard to beat La Bête humaine, *where Zola leaves us with that terrifying image of the driverless train hurtling to its destruction :*

Qu'importaient les victimes que la machine écrasait en chemin! N'allait-elle pas quand-même à l'avenir, insoucieuse du sang répandu? Sans conducteur, au milieu des ténèbres, en bête aveugle et sourde qu'on aurait lâchée parmi la mort, elle roulait, elle roulait, chargée de cette chair à canon, de ces soldats, déjà hébétés de fatigue, et ivres, qui chantaient.

But James Morris runs him close with the splendid line with which he concludes his book on Venice :

No wonder George Eliot's husband fell into the Grand Canal.

They noticed that virginity was needed
To trap the unicorn in every case,
But not that, of those virgins who succeeded,
A high percentage had an ugly face.

The hero was as daring as they thought him,
But his peculiar boyhood missed them all;
The angel of a broken leg had taught him
The right precaution to avoid a fall.

So in presumption they set forth alone
On what, for them, was not compulsory
And stuck half-way to settle in some cave
With desert lions to domesticity;

Or turned aside to be absurdly brave,
And met the ogre and were turned to stone.

From W. H. Auden,
The Quest

Long ago, reading Garrett Mattingly's The Defeat of the Spanish Armada, *I came across the following sentence about Dr – later Cardinal – William Allen :*

> Since he had left England William Allen had thoroughly learned, as another exile had learned before him, how steep the stairs are going up and down in strangers' houses, how bitter-salt the bread that exiles eat.

The extraordinary thing was that in those days I had no idea that the source was Dante, and that the images of the salty bread and the steep stairs were well known throughout the world. What Dante actually wrote, in Canto XVII of the Paradiso, *was :*

> Tu proverai si come sa di sale
>   Lo pane altrui, e come è duro calle
>   Lo scendere e 'l salir per l'altrui scale.

More recently, Mr David Rose of County Cork has drawn my attention to two other literary echoes of the same theme. The first is a quatrain from a poem called 'Famous Exiles', by H. W. Nevinson :

> And Dante up and down another's stairs,
> Abhorrent as the craggy depths of Hell,
> In exile climbed, though Rome's Imperial care
> Wrenched at his heart that was love's citadel.

The second is part of an occasional poem written in a visitors' book by J. L. Motley, and quoted in Henry Chaplin, a Memoir, *by Lady Londonderry :*

> Bitter the bread –
> So Dante said –
> One eats at strangers' banquets,
> And ill he fares
> Who goes upstairs
> To sleep in strangers' blankets.
> But I opine
> The Florentine,
> Who thus in strains heroic
> Bewailed his lot,
> Had quite forgot
> His sorrows at Glen Quoich.

I have since discovered a third, by Oscar Wilde :

> How steep the stairs within Kings' houses are
> For exile-wearied feet as mine to tread.

Wilde actually used this couplet twice – first in 'Ravenna' and again in his sonnet 'At Verona'. I wonder why ; it's not very good.

Outside our bay but quite near, the ruffle of the wind continued. One could see but not hear it making a noise, running its fingers through the blue and tangling it in waves. Safe in shelter, the *Elfin* gave a tiny movement now and then, of patience, like a sigh, or a horse standing that shifts from one foot to the other.

Freya Stark,
The Lycian Shore

J'aurais tué Pégase et je l'aurais fait cuire
Afin de vous offrir une aile de cheval...

Victor Hugo

More useful palindromes:

Now stop, Major-General: are Negro jampots won?

It is admittedly not easy to see in just what circumstances the above question might be asked. The next context is more readily imagined; what other words would spring to the lips when breaking the news of the death of a prize herd of cattle, suddenly smitten with infective epilepsy?

Stiff, O dairyman! In a myriad of fits!

Dr Barnardo making out the menus:

Desserts I desire not, so long no lost one rise distressed.

Finally, the rebuke of the high-principled lady to her rich Norman lover:

Diamond light, Odo, doth gild no maid.

On 3 September 1969, The Times *ran the following two announcements consecutively in its 'In Memoriam' column :*

OLIVER CROMWELL, 25th April, 1599 – 3rd September 1658. Lord Protector, 1653–1658. Statesman, General and Ruler.
  'Let God arise, let His enemies be scattered'.
                                              – Psalm 68, verse 1.
In honoured remembrance.

CROMWELL. – To the eternal condemnation of Oliver, Seditionist, Traitor, Regicide, Racialist, proto-Fascist and blasphemous Bigot. God save England from his like. – Hugo Ball.

At the marriage of his daughter to Rich, in November 1657, the Lord Protector threw about sack-posset among all the ladyes to soyle their rich cloaths, which they tooke as a favour, and also wett sweetmeats; and daubed all the stooles where they were to sit with wett sweetmeats; and pulled off Rich his peruque, and would have thrown it into the fire, but did not, yet he sate upon it.

From one of Richard Symons's pocket-books,
preserved among the
Harleian MSS. in the British Museum, No. 991

This 'Song of a Young Lady to her Ancient Lover' is in fact not by a young lady at all, but by John Wilmot, Earl of Rochester. But it is none the worse for that.

Ancient Person, for whom I
All the flattering Youth defy:
Long be it ere thou grow Old,
Aching, shaking, crazy Cold.
But still continue as thou art,
Ancient Person of my Heart.

On thy wither'd Lips and Dry
Which like barren Furrows lye,
Brooding Kisses I will pour
Shall thy Youthful Heat restore.
Such kind show'rs in Autumn fall,
And a Second Spring recall:
Nor from thee will ever part,
Ancient Person of my Heart.

Thy Nobler parts which but to name
In our Sex would be counted shame,
By Age's frozen grasp possest,
From their ice shall be releast:
And sooth'd by my reviving hand
In former warmth and vigour stand.
All a lover's wish can reach
For thy Joy my love shall teach.
And for thy Pleasure shall improve
All that Art can add to Love.
Yet still I love thee without Art,
Ancient Person of my Heart.

A
Christmas
Cracker

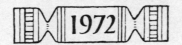

1972

From the Reminiscences *of Mrs Siddons I cannot resist quoting the following as an example of a royal compliment that might have been more happily turned:*

The Royal Family very frequently honoured me with their presence. The King [George III] was often moved to tears which he as often vainly endeavoured to conceal behind his eye-glass, and her Majesty the Queen at one time told me in her gracious broken English that her only refuge from me was actually turning her back upon the stage at the same time protesting 'It is indeed too disagreeable.' In short all went on most gloriously at the Theatre. . . .

But my favourite Mrs Siddons story comes from the diary of her companion, with whom she travelled to Wales in May 1802. Patty Wilkinson writes:

We left Conway next morning and ere long crossed Penman Maur, where, like other travellers, we alighted from our carriages to look from a bridge that commands the fullest view of the sublime landscape, with all its rocks and water. A lady within hearing of us was in such ecstasies, that she exclaimed, 'This awful scenery makes me feel as if I were only a worm, or a grain of dust, on the face of the earth.' Mrs Siddons turned round, and said, 'I feel very differently.'

Horace Walpole had a curious criticism:

When without motion, her arms are not genteel.

Life for him was an adventure; perilous indeed, but men are not made for safe havens.

Edith Hamilton on Aeschylus
(The Greek Way)

Dorothy Parker said much the same thing, equally beautifully, about Isadora Duncan:

There was never a place for her in the ranks of the terrible, slow army of the cautious. She ran ahead, where there were no paths.

Eothen, or Traces of Travel Brought Home from the East was first published in 1844 and remains one of my favourite travel books. Here Kinglake tells of the terrible moment when, riding across Sinai to Cairo, he suddenly spotted an Englishman, in an English shooting-jacket, bearing down from the opposite direction.

As we approached each other, it became with me a question whether we should speak; I thought it likely that the stranger would accost me, and in the event of his doing so, I was quite ready to be as sociable, and chatty as I could be, according to my nature, but still I could not think of anything particular that I had to say to him; of course among civilized people, the not having anything to say is no excuse at all for not speaking, but I was shy, and indolent, and I felt no great wish to stop, and talk like a morning visitor, in the midst of those broad solitudes. The traveller, perhaps, felt as I did, for except that we lifted our hands to our caps, and waved our arms in courtesy, we passed each other, as if we had passed in Bond Street. Our attendants, however, were not to be cheated of the delight that they felt in speaking to new listeners, and hearing fresh voices once more. The masters, therefore, had no sooner passed each other than their respective servants quietly stopped, and entered into conversation. As soon as my camel found that her companions were not following her, she caught the social feeling and refused to go on. I felt the absurdity of the situation, and determined to accost the stranger, if only to avoid the awkwardness of remaining stuck fast in the Desert, whilst our servants were amusing themselves. When with this intent I turned round my camel, I found that the gallant officer, who had passed me by about thirty or forty yards, was exactly in the same predicament as myself. I put my now willing camel in motion, and rode up towards the stranger, who, seeing this, followed my example, and came forward to meet me. He was the first to speak; he was much too courteous to address me as if he admitted the possibility of my wishing to accost him from any feeling of mere sociability, or civilian-like love of vain talk; on the contrary, he at once attributed my advances to a laudable wish of acquiring statistical information, and, accordingly, when we got within speaking distance, he said, 'I dare say, you wish to know how the Plague is going on at Cairo?' and then he went on to say, he regretted that his information did not enable him to give me in numbers a perfectly accurate statement of the daily deaths; he afterwards talked pleasantly enough upon other, and less ghastly subjects. I thought him manly, and intelligent – a worthy one of the few thousand strong Englishmen, to whom the Empire of India is committed.

Adam, a brown old vulture in the rain,
Shivered below his wind-whipped olive-trees;
Huddling sharp chin on scarred and scraggy knees,
He moaned and mumbled to his darkening brain;
'He was the grandest of them all – was Cain!
A lion laired in the hills, that none could tire;
Swift as a stag; a stallion of the plain,
Hungry and fierce with deeds of huge desire.'

Grimly he thought of Abel, soft and fair –
A lover with disaster in his face,
And scarlet blossom twisted in bright hair.
'Afraid to fight; was murder more disgrace? . . .
God always hated Cain . . .' He bowed his head –
The gaunt wild man whose lovely sons were dead.

Siegfried Sassoon

It is interesting to compare that sonnet by Sassoon with the following lines by Wilfred Owen. Both poets are haunted by the same theme – the carnage of the First World War in which they were both fighting – and both have found their inspiration in the Old Testament. But Owen goes deeper.

So Abram rose, and clave the wood, and went,
And took the fire with him, and a knife.
And as they sojourned both of them together,
Isaac the first-born spake and said, My Father,
Behold the preparations, fire and iron,
But where the lamb for this burnt-offering?
Then Abram bound the lad with belts and straps,
And builded parapets and trenches there,
And stretched forth the knife to slay his son.
When lo! an angel called him out of heaven,
Saying, Lay not thy hand upon the lad,
Neither do anything to him. Behold,
A ram, caught in a thicket by its horns;
Offer the Ram of Pride instead of him.
But the old man would not so, but slew his son –
And half the seed of Europe, one by one.

Un rien, un arbre, une fleur, un lézard, une tortue, provoquant le souvenir de mille métamorphoses chantées par les poètes; un filet d'eau, un petit creux dans le rocher qu'on qualifie d'antre des nymphes, un puits avec une tasse sur la margelle, un pertuis de mer si étroit que les papillons le traversent et pourtant navigable aux plus grands vaisseaux, comme à Poros; des orangers, des cyprès dont l'ombre s'étend sur la mer, un petit bois de pins au milieu des rochers, suffisent en Grèce pour produire le contentement qu'éveille la beauté.

Renan

Dictionary Definitions:

An extract from Liddell and Scott's Greek–English Lexicon. *I'm sure it must once have been familiar to every schoolboy, and now that the classics are less popular than they used to be I should hate it to be forgotten:*

ῥαφανιδόω: To thrust a radish up the fundament; a punishment for adulterers in Athens.

Another rich seam is J. G. Hava's Arabic–English Dictionary, published in Beirut as recently as 1964. Almost every entry gives additional proof – if such were needed – of the utter impossibility of the Arabic language.

جَون (*jawn*) Black. White. Light red. Day. Intensely black (horse).

خَال (*khàl*) Huge mountain. Big camel. Banner of a prince. Shroud. Fancy. Black stallion. Owner of a th. Self-magnified. Caliphate. Lonely place. Opinion. Suspicion. Bachelor. Good manager. Horse's bit. Liberal man. Weak-bodied, weak-hearted man. Free from suspicion. Imaginative man.

The first of these items elicited another nugget of information, from Professor Hugh Trevor-Roper, who called my attention to the fact that this improbable tradition was carried on by the Romans, who used not only radishes but also mullets. This is confirmed by Juvenal (Satire x 317) and also by Catullus, who ends his poem to Ausonius with the lines:

Ah! tum te miserum, malique fati,
Quem attractis pedibus, patente porta,
Percurrent raphanique, mugilesque.

The most extraordinary funerary monument I know is that of John Donne in the south aisle of St Paul's Cathedral. In his Life of Donne, *Izaak Walton tells the story :*

A monument being resolved upon, Dr Donne sent for a carver to make for him in wood the figure of an urn, giving him directions for the compass and height of it; and to bring with it a board, of the just height of his body. 'These being got, then without delay a choice painter was got to be in readiness to draw his picture, which was taken as followeth. – Several charcoal fires being first made in his large study, he brought with him into that place his winding-sheet in his hand, and having put off all his clothes, had this sheet put on him, and so tied with knots at his head and feet, and his hands so placed as dead bodies are usually fitted, to be shrowded and put into their coffin, or grave. Upon this urn he thus stood, with his eyes shut, and with so much of the sheet turned aside as might shew his lean, pale and death-like face, which was purposely turned towards the East, from whence he expected the second coming of his and our Saviour Jesus.' In this posture he was drawn at his just height; and when the picture was fully finished, he caused it to be set by his bedside, where it continued and became his hourly object till his death, and was then given to his dearest friend and executor Dr Henry King, then chief Residentiary of St Paul's, who caused him to be thus carved in one entire piece of white marble, as it now stands in that church.

Sir Henry Wotton, who knew Donne well, said of the statue :

It seems to breathe faintly, and posterity shall look upon it as a kind of artificial miracle.

Fortunately, resignation before approaching death can take other, less morbid forms. Consider for example the last words of Mirabeau. To his doctor-friend Cabanis he said:

Mon ami, je mourrai aujourd'hui. Quand on est là, il ne reste plus qu'une chose à faire; c'est de se parfumer, de se couronner de fleurs, et de s'environner de musique, afin d'entrer agréablement dans ce sommeil dont on ne réveille plus. Allons, qu'on se prépare à me raser, à faire ma toilette toute entière.

And then to Talleyrand:

On dit que la conversation est nuisible au malade; ce n'est pas celle-ci. On vivrait comme ça délicieusement, entouré de ses amis, et même on y meurt assez agréablement.

Consider, too, Madame du Deffand's farewell letter, written during her last illness, to Horace Walpole – whom, though she was eighty-four when she died and old enough to be his mother, she had loved deeply for fifteen years:

Divertissez-vous, mon ami, le plus que vous pourrez; ne vous affligez point de mon état; nous étions presque perdus l'un pour l'autre; nous ne nous devions jamais revoir; vous me regretterez, parce qu'on est bien aise de se savoir aimé.

In Brazilian Adventure, *Peter Fleming describes the public statuary of* Rio de Janeiro :

Victory has got a half-Nelson on Liberty from behind. Liberty is giving away about half a ton, and also carrying weight in the shape of a dying President and a brace of cherubs. (One of the cherubs is doing a cartwheel on the dying President's head, while the other, scarcely less considerate, attempts to pull his trousers off.) Meanwhile an unclothed male figure, probably symbolical, unquestionably winged, and carrying in one hand a model railway, is in the very act of delivering a running kick at the two struggling ladies, from whose drapery on the opposite side an eagle is escaping, apparently unnoticed. Around the feet of these gigantic principals all is bustle and confusion. Cavalry are charging, aboriginals are being emancipated and liners launched. Farmers, liberators, nuns, firemen and a poet pick their way with benign insouciance over a subsoil thickly carpeted with corpses, cannon-balls and scrolls. So vehement a confusion of thought, so arbitrary an alliance of ideas, takes the reason captive and paralyses criticism.

'And were you pleased?' they asked of Helen in Hell.
'Pleased?' answered she, 'when all Troy's towers fell;
And dead were Priam's sons, and lost his throne?
And such a war was fought as none had known;
And even the gods took part; and all because
Of me alone! Pleased?
                              I should say I was!'

                                    Lord Dunsany

Lord Byron's dog, Boatswain, was buried in the gardens of Newstead Abbey. His epitaph, which was once attributed to Byron himself but which we now know to have been written by Hobhouse, runs as follows:

Near this spot are deposited the remains of one who possessed Beauty without Vanity, Strength without Insolence, Courage without Ferocity, and all the Virtues of Man without his Vices. This praise, which would be unmeaning Flattery, if inscribed over human ashes, is but a just Tribute to the Memory of BOAT-SWAIN, a Dog.

My next favourite animal epitaph is that of Copenhagen, described on his tombstone as 'the charger ridden by the Duke of Wellington the entire day, at the Battle of Waterloo'. He was born in 1808 and died, after long years of honourable retirement, in 1836 at Stratfield Saye.

God's humbler instrument, though meaner clay,
Should share the glory of that glorious day.

Our predatory animal origin represents for mankind its last best hope. Had we been born of a fallen angel, then the contemporary predicament would lie as far beyond solution as it would lie beyond explanation. Our wars and our atrocities, our crimes and our quarrels, our tyrannies and our injustices could be ascribed to nothing other than singular human achievement. And we should be left with a clear-cut portrait of man as a degenerate creature endowed at birth with virtue's treasury whose only notable talent has been his capacity to squander it.

But we were born of risen apes, not fallen angels, and the apes were armed killers besides. And so what shall we wonder at? Our murders and massacres and missiles, and our irreconcilable regiments? Or our treaties whatever they may be worth; our symphonies, however seldom they may be played; our peaceful acres, however frequently they may be converted into battlefields; our dreams, however rarely they may be accomplished. The miracle of man is not how far he has sunk but how magnificently he has risen. We are known among the stars by our poems, not our corpses.

Robert Ardrey, African Genesis

Albrecht Dürer, writing from Venice on 7 February 1506:

Amongst the Italians I have many good friends who warn me not to eat or drink with their painters. Many of these are my enemies, and copy my work in the churches or wherever they can find it; and then they revile it and say that the style is not *antique* and therefore not good. Giovanni Bellini, however, has praised me highly to several gentlemen and wishes to have something of my doing; he called on me himself, and asked me to paint him a picture for which, he said, he would pay me well. People are all surprised that I should be so much thought of by a painter of his reputation: he is very old, but is still the best painter of them all.

The following specimen dialogue is taken from Hossfeld's New Practical Method for Learning the Spanish Language, by Tomás Enrique Gurrin, revised and enlarged by Fernando de Arteaga, Taylorian Teacher of Spanish in the University of Oxford. *Can it really, one wonders have been typical of the authors' conversation between themselves?*

Where has this come from?
It has come from my friend in Australia.

Why has he sent it?
In order to make you a present.

How far are you going?
I am going as far as Madrid.

Against whom does this bandit declare war?
Against the Government.

Who was versatile and ready-witted?
Ludovico Ariosto was.

Who availed himself of this licence, and where?
Marino in his Adonis.

Who was more strict to the precepts of art?
Torquato Tasso.

Where was the sweet harmony of voices raised?
Amid the din of battle.

What was it that fell?
The Roman Empire.

And what fell in her ruins?
Arts and sciences, as is usually the case.

Either you or your relatives have sold this estate.
Well, neither I nor my relatives sold it.

Somebody should start collecting the occasional verses of Evelyn Waugh. This neat little quatrain was prompted by an announcement in The Times *of 24 May 1957 that 'Lord Stanley of Alderley wishes to be addressed in the style of his senior Barony, Lord Sheffield' :*

Trusty as steel, more valuable than plate,
Aspiring Sheffield knocked at Heaven's gate.
Peter (who reads 'The Times') pronounced his doom,
Simply remarking 'Stanley, I presume.'

One of the inherent dangers in keeping a commonplace book is that of over-loading it with Pepys. Here he is on 5 December 1660:

... I dined at home; and after dinner went to the new Theatre and there I saw *The Merry Wifes of Windsor* acted. The humours of the Country gentleman and the French Doctor very well done; but the rest but very poorly, and Sir J. Falstaffe as bad as any.

From thence to Mr Will Montagu's chamber to have sealed some writings tonight between Sir R. Parkhurst and myself, about my Lord's 2000*l.*; but he not coming, I went to my father's. And there found my mother still ill of the stone and hath just newly voided one, which she hath let drop into the Chimny; and could not find it to show it me. From thence home and to bed.

It was not Shakespeare's only failure with Pepys. On 6 January 1663 he writes:

... And after dinner to the Dukes house and there saw *Twelfth night* acted well, though it be but a silly play and not relating at all to the name or day. Thence Mr Battersby (the apothecary), his wife and I and mine by coach together, and setting him down at his house, he paying his share, my wife and I home and find all well. Only, myself somewhat vexed at my wife's neglect in leaving of her scarfe, waistcoat, and night-dressings in the coach today that brought us from Westminster, though I confess she did give them to me to look after – yet it was her fault not to see that I did take them out of the coach.

Francesco Durante was a Neapolitan composer. He lived from 1684 to 1755.
In Grove's *Dictionary of Music and Musicians* Frank Walker *writes of*
him as follows:

Durante seems to have been a man of the utmost integrity, at once
simple and profoundly wise. We find him, in the records of the
Neapolitan conservatories, called in to compose the differences
between his more excitable colleagues. He was a great 'character',
who bore the sorrows and afflictions of his life with a positively super-
human equanimity. He was thrice married, the first time to a real
termagant, who lived for nothing but the lottery. She tried his
patience sorely, and he was obliged to work extremely hard, and
even deprive himself of sleep at nights, in order to earn enough to
enable her to satisfy her passion for gambling. He returned one day
from a journey to find she had sold all his compositions in manuscript. He sat down calmly and began the long task of writing them
out again from memory. At length death relieved him of this
encumbrance, and after a short time he married his servant, a
young girl *di bellissime forme*, whom he tenderly loved and with
whom he was very happy until she too died. The strength of
character he exhibited at this time was extraordinary. He arranged
and himself conducted the music for the funeral ceremony in his
home, after which, with tranquil resignation and without displaying
any sign of emotion, he lifted the body from the bed where it lay
and deposited it in the coffin. Then, having embraced his dead wife
for the last time, he covered her face with a piece of fine linen and
himself nailed down the coffin lid. He later married another of his
servants.

His simple manners were endearing. Always rather slovenly
dressed, he nevertheless attached considerable importance to his
wig, on which a good deal of his dignity depended. In order not to
disarrange it he would carry his three-cornered hat under his right
arm and would often be seen to stop in the streets and purchase
some fresh figs, which he put in his hat and consumed on the way
to the conservatory. He seems to have been fond of fruit: Paisiello
records that he died 'of a diarrhoea brought on by a feed of melons'.

It is – or was, before the appearance of the New English Bible – *refreshing to note that St Paul, though he usually spoke with the tongues of men and of angels, occasionally approximated more to the language of Nancy Mitford:*

How shall not the ministration of the spirit be rather glorious?

2 Corinthians 3:8

Many a time hath banished Norfolk fought
For Jesu Christ in glorious Christian field,
Streaming the ensign of the Christian cross
Against black pagans, Turks and Saracens,
And toil'd with works of war, retir'd himself
To Italy, and there at Venice gave
His body to that pleasant country's earth,
And his pure soul unto his captain Christ
Under whose colours he had fought so long.

Richard II, IV, i

I know of no lovelier obituary.

In the Hall of Corby Castle, Cumbria, there is to be seen an armorial plate, much re-tooled, quoting the first seven lines of the above (why not the last two?) and an additional inscription that reads:

The remains of the tomb of Thomas Mowbray, Duke of Norfolk, buried in the church of St Mark at Venice in Septr. 1399. Discovered and obtained by Rawdon Brown Esqr: and given by him to Henry Howard. It was saved from destruction by the zeal and device of Domenico Spiera when ordered to be destroyed in 1810.

Some time ago I discovered, tucked inside my father's copy of Through the Looking-Glass, *an autographed letter from the author. It is obviously addressed – despite the internal evidence ostensibly to the contrary – to a little girl. It strikes me as wonderfully characteristic – no one else could possibly have written it – but isn't it a bit sinister as well?*

March 30, 1861.
Ch. Ch. Oxford.

My dear Kathleen,

I promised once, if you remember, to send you one of these little penknives on your next birthday, and I hope this will arrive in time. I send with it my wishes for your good health, and many happy returns of your 72nd birthday. (Do not be surprised at my knowing your age: Henrietta told me, or I should never have guessed it, since you certainly do not look so old.) I hope you will find this knife as good as the one which you told me you lost about forty years ago.

I will tell you a few ways in which you will find it useful. First, you should cut your meat at dinner with it: in this way you will be safe from eating too much, and so making yourself ill. If you find that when the others have finished you have only had one mouthful, do not be vexed about it, but say to yourself '*I will eat quicker tomorrow.*' Then, when you go for a walk, if you hadn't this knife you might be in danger of tiring yourself by walking too far – but now, by simply making a rule always to *cut your name on every tree you come to*, I am sure you will never go far enough to do yourself any harm. Besides this, whenever you wish to punish your brothers, you will find it very convenient to do so by running the knife into their hands and faces (particularly the end of the nose); you will find it gives a good deal of pain if you run it in hard enough.

No doubt you will find out many other ways in which this knife will be useful, and I hope to hear that you like it, and always use it in the ways which I have mentioned. If you think of writing, (and mind you don't sign yourself 'K' again – I know no young lady of *that* name) my direction will be C. L. Dodgson Esq., J. Hunt Esq., Ore House, near Hastings till the 6th of April, and after that Ch. Ch. Oxford. So, my dear Kathleen, I remain

Your affte. friend
Charles L. Dodgson.

'Beautiful Truth!' exclaimed the Chorus, looking upward. 'How is your name profaned by vicious persons! You don't live in a well, my holy principle, but on the lips of false mankind. It is hard to bear with mankind, dear sir,' – addressing the elder Mr Chuzzlewit; 'but let us do so meekly. It is our duty so to do. Let us be among the Few who do their duty. If,' pursued the Chorus, soaring up into a lofty flight, 'as the poet informs us, England expects Every man to do his duty, England is the most sanguine country on the face of the earth, and will find itself continually disappointed.'

Martin Chuzzlewit

As a change from palindromes, try holorhymes – whole lines which have the same sound but different meanings. For some reason, they seem to go better in French. Louise de Vilmorin gave me two beautiful ones:

> Étonnamment monotone et lasse
> Est ton âme en mon automne, hélas!

and

> Gall, amant de la reine, alla, tour magnanime,
> Gallament de l'arène à la Tour Magne, à Nîmes.

This second one is by Victor Hugo. Some time ago an entrant in a New Statesman *competition made a bold stab at a translation. I noted it, but idiotically failed to note the author. If he sees this I hope he will forgive me:*

> Gall, doll-lover, 'ghost' to royalty at right hour,
> Galled all over, goes to royal tea at Rye Tower.

Here is another admirable one by Victor Hugo:

> O! fragiles Hébreux! Allez, Rébecca, tombe!
> Offre à Gilles zèbres, œufs; à l'Erèbe, hécatombe!

Finally, and shortest of all, there is the poem about Zeus when metamorphosed as a swan:

> Léda
> L'aida.

TO MUSICK, TO BECALM A SWEET-SICK YOUTH

Charms, that call down the moon from out her sphere,
On this sick youth work your enchantment here:
Bind up his senses with your numbers, so
As to entrance his paine, or cure his woe.
Fall gently, gently, and a while him keep
Lost in the civill Wildernesse of sleep:
That done, then let him, dispossest of paine,
Like to a slumbering Bride, awake againe.

Herrick

A
Christmas
Cracker

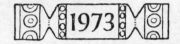

The following letter was written by Anthony Henley, Member of Parliament for Southampton from 1727 to 1734, to his constituents who had protested to him about the Excise Bill:

Gentlemen,

I received yours and am surprised by your insolence in troubling me about the Excise. You know, what I very well know, that I bought you. And I know, what perhaps you think I don't know, you are now selling yourselves to Somebody Else; and I know, what you do not know, that I am buying another borough. May God's curse light upon you all: may your houses be as open and common to all Excise Officers as your wifes and daughters were to me, when I stood for your scoundrell corporation.

Yours, etc.,
Anthony Henley

The text of this letter has been slightly corrected since it appeared in the 1973 Cracker, *thanks to the late Lord Henley who gave me the authentic version. He confirmed that the letter was written in 1734, in which year Henley, as his letter implies, ceased to represent Southampton. In the previous year, on 31 March, the* Weekly Register *had noted:*

Lady Betty Berkeley, daughter of the Earl of that name, being almost fifteen has thought it time to be married, and ran away last week with Mr Henley, a man noted for his impudence and immorality but a good estate and a beau.

Et sur elle courbé, l'ardent Impérator
Vit dans ses larges yeux étoilés de points d'or
Toute une mer immense où fuyaient des galères.

Hérédia

The last scene of James Elroy Flecker's Hassan – *which, I was surprised to discover, was first staged in Darmstadt of all places, in a German translation, with Frederick Valk in the name part – is set 'At the Gate of the Moon, Baghdad' in 'blazing moonlight'. It consists exclusively of the famous song 'The Golden Road to Samarkand', sung as the caravan makes ready to depart:*

> Sweet to ride forth at evening from the wells,
>   When shadows pass gigantic on the sand
> And softly through the silence beat the bells
>   Along the Golden Road to Samarkand.

Until a short time ago, my favourite verse had always been that sung by the Chief Grocer:

> We have rose-candy, we have spikenard,
>   Mastic and terebinth and oil and spice,
> And such sweet jams meticulously jarred
>   As God's Own Prophet eats in Paradise.

Recently, however, in Mr Wilfrid Blunt's book The Golden Road to Samarkand, *I have come across an additional verse which the author decided to omit, presumably thinking it somewhat too improper for contemporary audiences, or at least for the contemporary Lord Chamberlain. It can still be seen, crossed out, in the original manuscript, now in the Fitzwilliam Museum, Cambridge. It is given to a new personage, the Chief Humanist:*

> And we have boys and girls of special kinds,
>   White, brown and black, fragile or fair or strong;
> Their bosoms shame the roses: their behinds
>   Impel the astonished nightingales to song.

To be Catholic or Jewish isn't chic. Chic is Episcopalian.

Elizabeth Arden

(Or, to give her her real name, Florence Nightingale Graham.)

My first introduction to the diaries of Benjamin Constant was when I read Mistress to an Age, J. Christopher Herold's biography of Madame de Staël. Nearly all Constant's life with Germaine, at Coppet and elsewhere, is covered by these diaries, but

. . . only an abbreviated journal covers the period from 8 May 1805 to 12 April 1808. It is partly written in number code. The code tells more of Benjamin than anything else could do in so little space:

1 – Physical [i.e. sexual] pleasure.
2 – Desire to break my eternal chain [with Madame de Staël].
3 – Reconciliation with this bond, because of memories or a momentary charm.
4 – Work.
5 – Disputes with my father.
6 – Tenderness for my father.
7 – Travel projects.
8 – Marriage projects.
9 – Tired of Mrs Lindsay.
10 – Sweet memories and revival of love for Mrs Lindsay.
11 – Irresolution in my projects with regard to Mme du Tertre.
12 – Love for Mme du Tertre.
13 – Indecision about everything.
14 – Plan to settle at Dôle to break with Biondetta.
15 – Plan to settle in Lausanne for the same purpose.
16 – Projects for a voyage overseas.
17 – Desire to make up with certain enemies [i.e. Napoleon].

Numbers 9 and 10 gave Benjamin some slight trouble during his remaining weeks in Paris. On 3 July, after receiving a letter from Germaine which prompted him to write fourteen 2s in a row, he left for Coppet.

In 1850, Augustus Welby Pugin published his 'Remarks on Articles in the "Rambler"', in the course of which he wrote of his recent conversion to Roman Catholicism:

Oh! then, what delight! what joy unspeakable!... the stoups are filled to the brim; the rood is raised on high; the screen glows with sacred imagery and rich device; the niches are filled; the altar is replaced, sustained by sculptured shafts, the relics of saints repose beneath, the Body of Our Lord is enshrined on its consecrated stone; the lamps of the sanctuary burn bright; the saintly portraitures in the glass windows shine all gloriously; and the albs hang in the oaken ambries, and the cope chests are filled with orphreyed baudekins; and pix and pax, and chrismatory are there, and thurible and cross ...

Perhaps he was asking for it; anyway he got it – from Ruskin:

... But of all these fatuities, the basest is the being lured into the Romanist Church by the glitter of it, like larks into a trap by broken glass; to be blown into a change of religion by the whine of an organ-pipe; stitched into a new creed by gold threads on priests' petticoats; jangled into a change of conscience by the chimes of a belfry. I know nothing in the shape of error so dark as this, no imbecility so absolute, no treachery so contemptible. ...

The diatribe continues in similar vein ('Was it parsimony that you buried its paltry pinnacles in that eruption of diseased crockets?') in Appendix 12 to Vol. I of the first edition of The Stones of Venice. *Almost immediately after its publication in 1851, Pugin lost his reason and was confined in Bedlam, where he died the following year. Whether this fate was a direct consequence of the above cannot now be established; but Ruskin withdrew the whole passage from the second edition.*

RE-AWAKENING

The bugle calls across the desert waste.
Hearts quicken, bosoms pump. Our faith is not misplaced.
The winds of Africa blow, sweeping away all wrong.
Listen to me, O heroes, the burden of my song.
How Tyranny and Oppression with hideous face
Spat at the generous men (and women too) who make up this
splendid race.
Grip your fists, O sons of Khartoum,
Medani, Obeid, Fashir, Port Sudan, Kassala, Juba, Wau, all
round the historic tomb.

I am from the North, and I am far from home,
Yet my thoughts are with your thoughts, wherever I may roam.
You defeated them in the past, the invaders, Hicks,
You are always ready to get out of another fix.
Land of the tall Shilluk, the leggy Dinka,
Brothers of the North, skins black, brown, getting pinker.
O Mother of Heroes, true meaning of Umm-durman, give us
strength at this time,
Make their actions worthy of this humble rhyme.
Like the university crews, pulling together,
Get through even the worst of stormy weather.
Umma, N.U.P., Democrats, Communists, Moslem Brothers,
You are all Sudanese, by no means others,
Shoulder to shoulder, brothers of the Nile,
You will beat off all enemies, make them run many a mile.

Published in the Khartoum *Morning News*,
2 March 1965

Horace Walpole describes the funeral of George II in 1760:

When we came to the chapel of Henry the Seventh, all solemnity and decorum ceased; no order was observed, people sat or stood where they could or would; the yeomen of the guard were crying out for help, oppressed by the immense weight of the coffin; the Bishop read sadly, and blundered in the prayers; the fine chapter, *Man that is born of a Woman*, was chanted, not read; and the anthem, besides being immeasurably tedious, would have served as well for a nuptial. The real serious part was the figure of the Duke of Cumberland, heightened by a thousand melancholy circumstances. He had a dark brown adonis, and a cloak of black cloth, with a train of five yards. Attending the funeral of a father could not be pleasant: his leg extremely bad, yet forced to stand upon it near two hours; his face bloated and distorted with his late paralytic stroke, which has affected, too, one of his eyes, and placed over the mouth of the vault, into which, in all probability, he must himself so soon descend; think how unpleasant a situation! He bore it all with a firm and unaffected countenance. This grave scene was fully contrasted by the burlesque Duke of Newcastle. He fell into a fit of crying the moment he came into the chapel, and flung himself back in a stall, the Archbishop hovering over him with a smelling-bottle; but in two minutes his curiosity got the better of his hypocrisy, and he ran about the chapel with his glass to spy who was or was not there, spying with one hand, and mopping his eyes with the other. Then returned the fear of catching cold; and the Duke of Cumberland, who was sinking with heat, felt himself weighed down, and turning round, found it was the Duke of Newcastle standing upon his train, to avoid the chill of the marble.

Here, by contrast, is Benjamin Robert Haydon at the coronation of George IV on 19 July 1821 :

The appearance of a monarch has something in it like the rising of a sun. There are indications which announce the luminary's approach; a streak of light – the tipping of a cloud – the singing of the lark – the brilliance of the sky, till the cloud edges get brighter and brighter, and he rides majestically in the heavens. So with a king's advance. A whisper of mystery turns all eyes to the throne. Suddenly two or three rise; others fall back; some talk, direct, hurry, stand still, or disappear. Then three or four of high rank appear from behind the throne; an interval is left; the crowds scarce breathe. Something rustles, and a being buried in satin, feathers, and diamonds rolls gracefully into his scat. The room rises with a sort of feathered, silken thunder.

If only Haydon could have painted as well as he wrote . . .

A sixteenth-century tomb in York Minster bears the following epitaph:

Yf wisedome wealth honor or honesty
Chastity zeale faith hope or charity
If universall learning language law
Pure piety religion's reverend awe
Firm friends, fayre issue; if a virtuous wife,
A quiet conscience, a contented life,
The cleargies prayers or ye poor mans tears
Could have lent lenght to mans determined years
Sure as ye fate which for our fault wie feare
Proud death had nere advanced this tropie here.
In it behold thy doom, thy toombe provide;
Sir William Gee had all these pleas, yet died.

At Easter 1900, Oscar Wilde was in Rome. On Easter Monday he wrote to Robert Ross of his first sight of Pope Leo XIII:

He was wonderful as he was carried past me on his throne, not of flesh and blood, but a white soul robed in white, and an artist as well as a saint – the only instance in History, if the newspapers are to be believed.

I have seen nothing like the extraordinary grace of his gesture, as he rose, from moment to moment, to bless – possibly the pilgrims, but certainly me. Tree should see him. It is his only chance.

I was deeply impressed; and my walking-stick showed signs of budding. . . .

How did I get the ticket? By a miracle, of course. I thought it was hopeless, and made no effort of any kind. On Saturday afternoon at five o'clock Harold and I went to have tea at the Hôtel de l'Europe. Suddenly, as I was eating buttered toast, a man, or what seemed to be one, dressed like a hotel porter, entered and asked me would I like to see the Pope on Easter Day. I bowed my head humbly and said '*Non sum dignus*' or words to that effect. He at once produced a ticket!

When I tell you that his countenance was of supernatural ugliness, and that the price of the ticket was thirty pieces of silver, I need say no more.

Previous Crackers *have included palindromes and holorhymes; now it's the turn of mnemonics. All the best ones should enable one to remember basically useless information – still more useless, ideally, than the first thirty-six Roman Emperors. Paddy Leigh-Fermor gave me the first two lines; and some time afterwards, lying in bed with a cold, I made up the rest.*

> A truant calf calls noisily;
> Great obstinate! Vile veal!
> Thus dominating nervousness
> Through hoarding apple-peel.
> Mid-August come, persistently,
> Don-Juans, sex-suffused,
> Coerce mature hetairas
> Anti-socially misused.
> Go, go, my boys! Go pandering!
> Descend green Arno's valley!
> Give chase! Among those flowery peaks
> Can't countless numbers dally?

The initial letters give the key to the Emperors:

Augustus, Tiberius, Caligula, Claudius, Nero,
Galba, Otho, Vitellius, Vespasian,
Titus, Domitian, Nerva,
Trajan, Hadrian, Antoninus Pius,
Marcus Aurelius, Commodus, Pertinax,
Didius Julianus, Septimius Severus,
Caracalla, Macrinus, Heliogabalus,
Alexander Severus, Maximin,
Gordian, Gordian, Maximus, Balbinus, Gordian, Philip,
Decius, Gallus, Aemilianus, Valerian,
Gallienus, Claudius, Aurelian, Tacitus, Florianus, Probus,
Carus, Carinus, Numerian, Diocletian.

This poem was written by a fifteen-year-old boy two years before he committed suicide. Grim fare, you may think, for a Christmas Cracker; but it deserves to be better known and this is one way of making it so.

Once . . . he wrote a poem.
And he called it 'Chops',
Because that was the name of his dog, and
        that's what it was all about.
And the teacher gave him an 'A'
And a gold star.
And his mother hung it on the kitchen door,
        and read it to all his aunts . . .

Once . . . he wrote another poem.
And he called it 'Question Marked Innocence',
Because that was the name of his grief, and
        that's what it was all about.
And the professor gave him an 'A'
And a strange and steady look.
And his mother never hung it on the kitchen door
        because he never let her see it . . .

Once, at 3 a.m. . . . he tried another poem . . .
And he called it absolutely nothing, because
        that's what it was all about.
And he gave himself an 'A'
And a slash on each damp wrist,
And hung it on the bathroom door because he
        couldn't reach the kitchen.

Like Pepys, John Aubrey makes compulsive quoting. Here he is on Ben Jonson – whose name he spells, incidentally, in just about every possible way:

A Grace by Ben Johnston, extempore, before King James:

Our King and Queen the Lord-God blesse,
The Paltzgrave and the Lady Besse,
And God blesse every living thing
That lives, and breath's, and loves the King.
God bless the Councell of Estate,
And Buckingham the fortunate.
God blesse them all, and keepe them safe,
And God blesse me, and God blesse Raph.

The King was mighty enquisitive to know who this Raph was. Ben told him 'twas the Drawer at the Swanne Tavernne by Charing-Crosse, who drew him good Canarie . . .

When B.J. was dyeing King Charles sent him but **x** pounds.

He lies buried in the north aisle in the path of square stone (the rest is Lozenge) opposite to the Scutcheon of Robertus de Ros, with this Inscription only on him, in a pavement square of blew marble, about 14 inches square,

O RARE BENN JOHNSON

which was donne at the charge of Jack Young, afterwards knighted, who, walking there when the grave was covering, gave the fellow eighteen pence to cut it.

It is the Chinese and Japanese who are usually considered the greatest masters of concision in poetry; but as far as I'm concerned the palm goes to the anonymous Frenchman responsible for the following quatrain on the subject of Lot and his daughters:

Il but,
Il devint tendre:
Et puis il fut
Son gendre.

*Of all the sonnets I know, perhaps the oddest are these two by Leigh Hunt.
And yet, the more I read them, the better they seem to be.*

TO A FISH

You strange, astonished-looking, angle-faced,
  Dreary-mouthed, gaping wretches of the sea,
  Gulping salt water everlastingly,
Cold-blooded, though with red your blood be graced,
And mute, though dwellers in the roaring waste;
  And you, all shapes beside, that fishy be –
  Some round, some flat, some long, all devilry,
Legless, unloving, infamously chaste: –
O scaly, slippery, wet, swift, staring wights,
What is't ye do? What life lead? Eh, dull goggles?
How do ye vary your vile days and nights?
How pass your Sundays? Are ye still but joggles
In ceaseless wash? Still nought but gapes, and bites,
And drinks, and stares, diversified with boggles?

A FISH REPLIES

Amazing monster! that, for aught I know,
  With the first sight of thee didst make our race
  For ever stare! O flat and shocking face,
Grimly divided from the breast below!
Thou that on dry land horribly dost go
  With a split body and most ridiculous pace,
  Prong after prong, disgracer of all grace,
Long-useless-finned, haired, upright, unwet, slow!
O breather of unbreathable, sword-sharp air,
  How canst exist? How bear thyself, thou dry
And dreary sloth? What particle canst share
  Of the only blessed life, and watery?
I sometimes see of ye an actual *pair*
  Go by, linked fin by fin, most odiously.

In a third, non-partisan sonnet, a Spirit sums up. It ends:

Man's life is warm, glad, sad, 'twixt loves and graves,
  Boundless in hope, honoured with pangs austere,
Heaven-gazing; and his angel-wings he craves: –
  The fish is swift, small-needing, vague yet clear,
A cold, sweet, silver life, wrapped in round waves,
  Quickened with touches of transporting fear.

I never tire of stories about Queen Victoria. There is a splendidly character-istic one in My Memories of Six Reigns *by Princess Marie Louise – a conversation which occurred shortly after the death of the Queen's son-in-law, Prince Henry of Battenberg, in 1896.*

On this particular afternoon to which I refer – a dark, dank after-noon in February – the Queen was at Osborne, and she went out for her customary drive with Lady Errol, who was then in waiting. These dear, elderly ladies, swathed in crêpe, drove in an open carriage, called a sociable. The Queen was very silent, and Leila (Lady Errol) thought it time to make a little conversation. So she said, 'Oh, Your Majesty, think of when we shall see our dear ones again in Heaven!'

'Yes,' said the Queen.

'We will all meet in Abraham's bosom,' said Leila.

'I will *not* meet Abraham,' said the Queen.

An entry in Queen Victoria's diary for this day runs: 'Dear Leila, not at all consolatory in moments of trouble!'

Nor does Abraham seem to be the only biblical patriarch to be incurring the Queen's continued displeasure. In his diary, on 15 March 1907, Wilfrid Scawen Blunt reports:

M., who came to luncheon, told an amusing story about the late Queen Victoria, who when there was talk about meeting dead people in another world was huffed at the idea of allowing King David to be presented to her on account of his 'inexcusable conduct to Uriah'.

For of the Gods we believe, and of men we know, that by a law of their nature wherever they can rule they will. This law was not made by us, and we are not the first who have acted upon it; we did but inherit it, and shall bequeath it to all time, and we know that you and all mankind, if you were as strong as we are, would do as we do.

The Athenians to the Melians,
in Thucydides' *History of the Peloponnesian War*
(tr. Jowett), v, 105

In the early years of the rule of General Amin in Uganda – the years when he was still a joke – stories about him always used to remind me of a curious little poem by Victor Hugo. It is called 'Pourboire Royal'.

J'allai faire visite au roi. Les avenues
De son palais étaient pleines de femmes nues,
Espèce de sérail épars comme un troupeau.
Quand j'entrai, le roi vint, coiffé d'un grand chapeau,
En habit noir, pieds nus, et complètement ivre,
Il s'assit sur un trône en cuir à clous de cuivre,
Et dit: Homme, sais-tu que je suis petit-fils
Du mage Zoroastre, ancien roi de Memphis?
Parle. – Et je répondis au fils de Zoroastre:
– Oui, sire. – Et je lui mis dans la main une piastre
Qu'il fourra prestement dans son frac de gala.
Il fut content, m'offrit à boire, et s'en alla.

For that same sweet sin of lechery, I would say as the Friar said:
A young man and a young woman in a green arbour in a May
morning – if God do not forgive it, I would.

Sir John Harington

After Akcha, the colour of the landscape changed from lead to aluminium, pallid and deathly, as if the sun had been sucking away its gaiety for thousands and thousands of years; for this was now the plain of Balkh, and Balkh they say is the oldest city in the world. The clumps of green trees, the fountain-shaped tufts of coarse cutting grass, stood out almost black against this mortal tint. Sometimes we saw a field of barley; it was ripe, and Turkomans, naked to the waist, were reaping it with sickles. But it was not brown or gold, telling of Ceres, of plenty. It seemed to have turned prematurely white, like the hair of a madman – to have lost its nourishment. And from these acred cerements, first on the north and then on the south of the road, rose the worn grey-white shapes of bygone architecture, mounds, furrowed and bleached by the rain and sun, wearier than any human works I ever saw: a twisted pyramid, a tapering platform, a clump of battlements, a crouching beast, all familiars of the Bactrian Greeks, and of Marco Polo after them. They ought to have vanished. But the very impact of the sun, calling out the obstinacy of their ashen clay, has conserved some inextinguishable spark of form, a spark such as a Roman earthwork or a grass-grown barrow has not, which still flickers on against a world brighter than itself, tired as only a suicide frustrated can be tired.

Robert Byron,
The Road to Oxiana

W. S. Gilbert, beginning a letter of complaint to the station-master at Baker Street, on the Metropolitan line:

Sir,
    Saturday morning, although recurring at regular and well-foreseen intervals, always seems to take this railway by surprise.

The following is an extract from a synopsis of Carmen, *thoughtfully provided some years ago by the Paris Opera for the benefit of its English and American patrons:*

Carmen is a cigar-makeress from a tabago factory who loves with Don José of the mounting guard. Carmen takes a flower from her corsets and lances it to Don José (Duet: 'Talk me of my mother'). There is a noise inside the tabago factory and the revolting cigar-makeresses bursts into the stage. Carmen is arrested and Don José is ordered to mounting guard her but Carmen subduces him and he lets her escape.

ACT 2. The Tavern. Carmen, Frasquita, Mercedes, Zuniga, Morales. Carmen's aria ('the sistrums are tinkling'). Enter Escamillio, a balls-fighter. Enter two smuglers (Duet: 'We have in mind a business') but Carmen refuses to penetrate because Don José has liberated from prison. He just now arrives (Aria: 'Slop, here who comes!') but hear are the bugles singing his retreat. Don José will leave and draws his sword. Called by Carmen shrieks the two smuglers interfere with her but Don José is bound to dessert, he will follow into them (final chorus: 'Opening sky wandering life'). . . .

AXT 4, a place in Seville. Procession of balls-fighters, the roaring of the balls heard in the arena. Escamillio enters, (Aria and chorus: 'Toreador, toreador, All hail the balls of a Toreador'.) Enter Don José (ARIA: 'I do not threaten, I besooch you'.) but Carmen repels himwants to join with Escamillio now chaired by the crowd. Don José stabbs her (Aria: 'Oh rupture, rupture, you may arrest me, I did kill der') he sings 'Oh my beautiful Carmen, my subductive Carmen. . . .'

FAREWELL TO JULIET

How shall I round the ending of a story,
   Now the wind's falling and the harbour nears?
How shall I sign your tiny Book of Glory,
   Juliet, my Juliet, after many years?

I'll sign it, One that halted at a Vision:
   One whom the shaft of beauty struck to flame:
One that so wavered in a strong decision:
   One that was born perhaps to fix your name.

One that was pledged, and goes to his replevining:
   One that now leaves you with averted face,
A shadow passing through the doors at evening
   To his companion and his resting place.

Hilaire Belloc

A
Christmas
Cracker

Two pieces of advice for foreign travellers:

In the matter of language it is always best to go to a little more trouble and learn the exact equivalent if possible. 'I am an Englishman and require instant attention to the damage done to my solar topee' is far better than any equivocation that may be meant well but will gain little respect.

Guide to the Native Languages of Africa,
by A Gentleman of Experience, 1890

An attenuation is often understood better than a circumlocution. *Exempli gratia:*

'Why is there no marmalade available?' is better understood in the form '*Quelle marmalade non?*'. 'Bring marmalade' may be simply rendered as '*Marmalade demandez*', always remembering that the z is silent as in 'deman*day*'. The little English joke about jam may be easily translated if one wishes to amuse the proprietor: '*Hier, marmalade; demain, marmalade; mais jamais marmalade de jour.*' Such little pleasantries are often appreciated.

French for the English,
by A Gentleman of Quality, 1894

There was a blind man – blind from birth – called W. H. Coates. He was a poet, and a remarkable one, for he had the unique gift of being able to describe landscape in tactile terms such as the blind can understand. In his book The World through Blunted Sight, *Patrick Trevor-Roper gives us his 'tactile' translation of ten lines from* Prometheus Unbound. *Shelley's original runs thus:*

> The point of one white star is quivering still
> Deep in the orange light of widening morn
> Beyond the purple mountains: through a chasm
> Of wind-divided mist the darker lake
> Reflects it; now it wanes; it gleams again
> As the waves fade, and as the burning threads
> Of woven cloud unravel in pale air:
> 'Tis lost! And through yon peaks of cloudlike snow
> The roseate sunlight quivers . . .

Coates translates:

> One cold metallic grain is quivering still
> Deep in the flood of warm ethereal fluid
> Beyond the velvet mountains: through a chasm
> In banks of fleece the heavier lake is splashed
> With flakes of fiery foam; it wanes, it grows
> As the waves thicken, and as the burning threads
> Of woven wool unravel in tepid air;
> 'Tis lost! And through the unsubstantial snow
> Of yonder peaks quivers the living form
> And vigour of the sun . . .

And now here is Gibbon on the first – and false – Pope John XXIII. The events described occurred in May 1415, five months before the battle of Agincourt.

Of the three [simultaneous] popes, John the Twenty-third was the first victim: he fled and was brought back a prisoner: the most scandalous charges were suppressed; the vicar of Christ was only accused of piracy, murder, rape, sodomy, and incest; and after subscribing his own condemnation he expiated in prison the imprudence of trusting his person to a free city beyond the Alps.

As things turned out, he didn't do too badly after all. Two years later, he was made a cardinal again; and when he died in 1419 he was buried in the Baptistery in Florence, with Donatello designing his tomb.

Every French schoolboy has heard of – and probably tried his hand at – the famous 'Dictée' which Prosper Mérimée set one evening to the court of Napoleon III, at Fontainebleau. According to the memoirs of Princess Pauline Metternich, the winner was Prince Metternich, with only three mistakes; then came Octave Feuillet with nineteen, Alexandre Dumas with twenty-four, Princess Metternich herself with forty-two, the Emperor with forty-five and the Empress Eugénie with sixty-two – not bad, it was thought, for a Spaniard. The text runs as follows:

Pour parler sans ambiguïté, ce dîner à Sainte-Adresse, près du Havre, malgré les effluves embaumés de la mer, malgré les vins de très bon crus, les cuisseaux de veau et les cuissots de chevreuil prodigués par l'amphitryon, fut un vrai guêpier.

Quelles que soient, et quelque exiguës qu'aient pu paraître, à côté de la somme due, les arrhes qu'étaient censés avoir données à maints et maints fusiliers subtils la douairière ainsi que le marguillier, bien que lui ou elle soit censée les leur avoir refusées et s'en soit repentie, va-t'en les réclamer pour telle ou telle bru jolie par qui tu les diras redemandées, quoiqu'il ne siée pas de dire qu'elle se les est laissé arracher par l'adresse desdits fusiliers et qu'on les leur aurait suppléées dans toute autre circonstance ou pour des motifs de toutes sortes.

Il était infâme d'en vouloir pour cela à ces fusiliers jumeaux et mal bâtis, et de leur infliger une raclée, alors qu'ils ne songeaient qu'à prendre des rafraîchissements avec leurs coreligionnaires.

Quoi qu'il en soit, c'est bien à tort que la douairière, par un contre-sens exorbitant, s'est laissé entraîner à prendre un râteau et qu'elle s'est crue obligée de frapper l'exigeant marguillier sur son omoplate vieillie.

Deux alvéoles furent brisés; une dysenterie se déclara, suivie d'une phtisie.

– Par Saint-Martin, quelle hémorragie! – s'écria ce bélître.

A cet événement, saisissant son goupillon, ridicule excédent de bagage, il la poursuivit dans l'église tout entière.

In the gallery of St Mary's Church, Paddington Green, now superbly restored, there is a memorial plaque which reads:

Near this Place lie the Remains of
John Christian Backhouse
First born Son of
John and Catherine Backhouse
of the parish of St. Margaret, Westminster.
He was a Child of Exiguous Beauty of Form
and he had a Precociousness of Intellect
of a Character probably Unparallelled.

.　.　.　.　.　,

He died on the 12th of May 1817
aged only Nine Months and 19 Days.

What is the most boring anecdote in literature? My own personal palm would go, I think, to the following extract from George Borrow's Wild Wales. *Of Llansilio church he writes:*

In the churchyard is a tomb in which an old squire of the name of Jones was buried about the middle of the last century. There is a tradition about this squire and tomb to the following effect. After the squire's death there was a lawsuit about his property, in consequence of no will having been found. It was said that his will had been buried with him in the tomb, which after some time was opened, but with what success the tradition sayeth not.

Nobody ever talked more and better sense than H. W. Fowler in his Modern English Usage. *Here is some of it.*

Mahomet, Mohammedan, &c. Before making any statement on these words, I asked a middle-aged lady whom she understood by the Prophet of Allah; she hesitated, suspecting some snare, but being adjured to reply said quite plainly that he was *Mahomet* (mā'ǫmĕt), & further called his followers Mahometans (mạ-hŏ'mĭ-tạnz) – thus fulfilling expectations. The popular forms are Mahomet(an) (mā'ǫmĕt *or* mạ-hŏ'mĭt, mạ-hŏ'mĭtn); the prevailing printed forms are Mohammed(an).

The worst of letting the learned gentry bully us out of our traditional *Mahometan* & *Mahomet* (who ever heard of *Mohammed & the Mountain?*) is this: no sooner have we tried to be good & learnt to say, or at least write, Mohammed than they are fired with zeal to get us a step or two further on the path of truth, which at present seems likely to end in *Muḥammad* with a dot under the h; *see* DIDACTICISM, PRIDE OF KNOWLEDGE. The literary, as distinguished from the learned, surely do good service when they side with tradition & the people against science & the dons. *Muḥammad* should be left to the pedants, *Mohammed* to historians & the like, while ordinary mortals should go on saying, & writing in newspapers & novels & poems & such general reader's matter, what their fathers said before them.

The fact is that we owe no thanks to those who discover, & cannot keep silence on the discovery, that *Mahomet* is further than *Mohammed*, and *Mohammed* further than *Muḥammad*, from what his own people called him. The Romans had a hero whom they spoke of as *Aeneas*; we call him that too, but for the French he has become *Énée*; are the French any worse off than we on that account? It is a matter of like indifference in itself whether the English for the Prophet's name is *Mahomet* or *Mohammed*; in itself, yes; but whereas the words *Aeneas* & *Énée* have the Channel between them to keep the peace, *Mahomet* & *Mohammed* are for ever at loggerheads; we want one name for the one man; & the one should have been that around which the ancient associations cling. It is too late to recover unity; the learned, & their too docile disciples, have destroyed that, & given us nothing worth having in exchange.

Nowadays, thanks to broadcasting, the gramophone and a general raising of standards, we are seldom forced to sit through excruciating musical performances of the kind that our grandparents knew. On the rare occasions when it does happen, these lines of Coleridge tend to come into my mind:

> Nor cold, nor stern, my soul! yet I detest
> These scented rooms where, to a gaudy throng,
> Heaves the proud harlot her distended breast
> In intricacies of laborious song.

One person who knew better than most how to deal with such a situation was Lady Lawless, the British Ambassadress in Rome in Maurice Baring's novel C. After the third song at some hideous Embassy entertainment, she was on her feet and at the singer's side.

'I like that one best of *all*,' she said, 'and *how* kind of you to have been able to spare us a moment tonight, and to have given us *all* such a treat, and to have sung *so* many songs. I do hope it hasn't *tired* you; you must take care of that precious throat. The Ambassador has so enjoyed it; we *all* have, and you must come to tea and sing another song very soon.' And as she talked she took Miss Sims's music from the pianoforte, and rolled it up neatly in a *rouleau*, and tied it with a little piece of pink ribbon, and presented it to her with a charming but completely final bow, and calling Herbert Napier she said to him, 'Mr Napier, will you take Miss Sims to have a cup of tea and some lemonade?' And so saying, she led the guests back to the drawing-room, and Napier conducted Miss Sims to a small buffet on the top of the staircase, where there were refreshments, whence she was ultimately shown out.

'She may do for concerts in England,' said Lady Lawless. 'One never knows what English people will like.'

Nor, it seems, was the problem entirely unknown in ancient Rome. There is a satire of Horace which begins:

Omnibus hoc vitium est cantoribus, inter amicos
Ut numquam inducant animum cantare rogati;
Injussi numquam desistant. . . .

(It is a failing of all singers, that if asked to sing among friends they can never be made to do so; unasked, they never stop.)

Cleopatra's lovely speech on the dead Antony:

> For his bounty,
> There was no winter in't; an autumn 'twas
> That grew the more by reaping: his delights
> Were dolphin-like, they showed his back above
> The element they liv'd in.

In the year A.D. *1000 the Western Emperor Otto III opened up the tomb of Charlemagne at Aix-la-Chapelle. He was accompanied by two bishops, and by Count Otto of Lomello, who left the following account (recorded by a chronicler in the monastery of Novalese in Lombardy):*

We entered in unto Charles. He was not lying down, as is the manner with the bodies of other dead men, but was sitting as though he were alive, on a chair. He was crowned with a golden crown and held a sceptre in his hands, the same being covered with gloves, through which the nails had grown. And above and around him was a tabernacle of brass and marble. Now when we were come into the tomb, we broke this down to make an opening in it. And when we entered in, we were assailed by a pungent smell. And so we sank upon our bended knees before him; and straightway Otto the Emperor clad him in white raiment, and cut his nails, and made good all that was lacking about him. But no part of his body had corrupted or fallen away, except a little piece of the end of his nose, which the Emperor caused at once to be restored with gold; and he took from his mouth one tooth, and built up the tabernacle again, and departed.

I love all waste
And solitary places, where we taste
The pleasure of believing what we see
Is boundless, as we wish our souls to be:
And such was this wide ocean, and this shore
More barren than its billows.

Shelley

I am indebted to Kensington Davison for this extract from what must be one of the most nauseating works of literature ever published – The Fragrant Minute for Every Day *by Wilhelmina Stitch.*

THE LADY BABY

On November 14 the wife of —————— *gave to the world a dear little lady baby.* – Birth Announcement.

'A Lady Baby came today.' What words are quite so nice to say? They make one smile, they make one pray for Lady Baby's happiness. 'Today a Lady Baby came.' We have not heard her winsome name, we can address her all the same as Lady Baby-Come-to-Bless.

When Lady Baby came to earth, her home was filled with joy and mirth. There's not a jewel of half the worth of Lady Baby-to-Caress. We're glad that Lady Baby's here, for at this sunless time of year there's naught that brings such warmth and cheer as Lady Baby's daintiness.

Hush! Lady Baby's fast asleep, the friendly fire-flames dance and leap and angels' wings above her sweep as on her eyes a kiss they press. 'A Lady Baby!' Lovely phrase, it means she'll have such gentle ways, and grow to goodness all her days – may God this Lady Baby bless!

On 16 March 1815, at four o'clock in the afternoon, Napoleon arrived at the Hôtel de la Poste at Avallon – which still stands – on his triumphant progress from Elba to Paris. At the same moment Louis XVIII called a joint meeting of the Assemblies in the Palais-Bourbon. He was wearing the Cross of the Légion d'Honneur for the first time; and the troops that were drawn up around the courtyard in the pelting rain, forced to shout 'Vive le Roi!', were muttering '. . . de Rome' under their breath.

Chateaubriand was there, and wrote:

> Louis XVIII monte lentement à son trône; les princes, les maréchaux et les capitaines des gardes se rangent aux deux côtés du Roi. Les cris cessent; tout se tait: dans cet intervalle de silence, on croyait entendre les pas lointains de Napoléon.

In the evening walked sadly along the shore of the Solent, east-wards by Pylewell – returning, brought home a glow-worm and put it in a white lily, through which it shone.

From the diary of William Allingham,
28 June 1863

While taking a parting cup of coffee with the postmaster I unluckily set my foot on a handsome pipe-bowl (pipe-bowls are always snares to near-sighted people moving over Turkish floors, as they are scattered in places quite remote from the smokers, who live at the farther end of the prodigiously long pipe-sticks) – crash; but nobody moved; only on apologizing through Giorgio, the polite Mohammedan said: 'The breaking of such a pipe-bowl would indeed, under ordinary circumstances, be disagreeable; but in a friend every action has its charm!'

Edward Lear, *Journals of a Landscape Painter
in Greece and Albania*, 1851

'Tis the Arabian bird alone
Lives chaste, because there is but one.
But had kind Nature made them two,
They would like doves and sparrows do.

Rochester

Lady Mary Wortley Montagu wrote from Thrace in 1717:

The summer is already far advanced in this part of the world; and, for some miles around Adrianople, the whole ground is laid out in gardens, and the banks of the river set with fruit trees, under which all the most considerable Turks divert themselves every evening; not with walking, that is not one of their pleasures, but a set party of them choose out a green spot, where the shade is very thick, and there they spread a carpet, on which they sit drinking their coffee, and generally attended by some slave with a fine voice, or that plays on some instrument. Every twenty paces you may see one of these little companies listening to the dashing of the river; and this taste is so universal, that the very gardeners are not without it. I have often seen them and their children sitting on the banks, and playing on a rural instrument, perfectly answering the description of the ancient *fistula*, being composed of unequal reeds, with a simple but agreeable softness in the sound.

Mr Addison might here make the experiment he speaks of in his travels; there not being one instrument of music among the Greek or Roman statues, that is not to be found in the hands of the people of this country. The young lads generally divert themselves with making garlands for their favourite lambs, which I have often seen painted and adorned with flowers, lying at their feet while they sung or played. It is not that they ever read romances, but these are the ancient amusements here, and as natural to them as cudgel-playing and football to our British swains; the softness and warmth of the climate forbidding all rough exercises, which were never so much as heard of amongst them, and naturally inspiring a laziness and aversion to labour, which the great plenty indulges. These gardeners are the only happy race of country people in Turkey. They furnish all the city with fruit and herbs, and seem to live very easily. They are most of them Greeks, and have little houses in the midst of their gardens, where their wives and daughters take a liberty not permitted in the town, I mean go unveiled. These wenches are very neat and handsome, and pass their time at their looms under the shade of the trees.

Love without hope, as when the young bird-catcher
Swept off his tall hat to the Squire's own daughter,
So let the imprisoned larks escape and fly
Singing about her head, as she rode by.

Robert Graves

I have recently come upon a book called Health's Improvement: Or, Rules Comprizing and Discovering the Nature, Method, and Manner of Preparing all sorts of FOOD used in this Nation. *It was written by 'that ever Famous Thomas Muffett, Doctor in Physick', but the 1655 edition has been 'corrected and enlarged' by one Christopher Bennet, similarly qualified and, in addition, Fellow of the 'Colledg of Physitians' in London. In the seventh chapter we read the following:*

> *St Genovese*, the holy Maid of *Paris* . . . (like the Egyptian prophetess) abstained wholly from flesh, because it is the mother of lust: she would eat no milk, because it is white blood: she would eat no eggs, because they are nothing but liquid flesh: thus pining and consuming her body both against nature and godliness, she lived in a foolish error, thinking flesh more ready to inflame lust, than fruit or fish, the contrary whereof is proved by the Islanders, Groenlanders, Orites, and other Nations; who feeding upon nothing but fish (for no beast nor fruit can live there for cold) yea having no other bread than is made of dried Stockfish grinded into powder, are nevertheless both exceeding lecherous, and also their women very fruitfull. Yea *Venus* the mother of lust and lechery is said to have sprung from the fome of fish, and to have been born in the Sea, because nothing is more availeable to engender lust, than the eating of certain fishes and sea-plants, which I had rather in this lascivious age to conceal from posterity, than to specifie them unto my Countrymen, as the *Grecians* and *Arabians* have done to theirs.

Dr Muffett, M.D.Basel, F.R.C.P. (1553–1604) has been unfairly upstaged by his daughter Patience, whose unfortunate encounter with a spider has passed into legend. It is odd that she should have been so disconcerted, since her father was even more distinguished as an entomologist than he was as a dietician. His book The Theatre of Insects, or Lesser Living Creatures – *posthumously published, as was* Health's Improvement – *was for many years the standard work on the subject.*

Un petit coup au carreau, comme si quelque chose l'avait heurté, suivi d'une ample chute légère comme de grains de sable qu'on eût laissés tomber d'une fenêtre au-dessus, puis la chute s'étendant, se réglant, adoptant un rhythme, devenant fluide, sonore, musicale, innombrable, universelle: c'était la pluie.

Proust,
Du Côté de chez Swann

And two conversations with Dr Johnson – from Boswell's account of the Tour to the Hebrides.

We talked of memory and its various modes.

JOHNSON. 'Memory will play strange tricks. One sometimes loses a single word. I once lost *fugaces* in the ode "Posthume, Posthume".'

I mentioned to him that a worthy gentleman of my acquaintance actually forgot his own name.

JOHNSON. 'Sir, that was a morbid oblivion.'

JOHNSON. '... There's as much charity in helping a man downhill as in helping him uphill.' BOSWELL. 'I don't think there's as much charity.' JOHNSON. 'Yes, sir, if his *tendency* be downwards. Till he's at bottom, he flounders. Get him to it, and he's quiet. Swift tells that Stella had a trick, which she learnt from Addison, to encourage a very absurd man in absurdity, rather than strive to pull him out of it.'

Two thoughts about pictures. First, by Kuo Hsi, a painter of the Sung period, born about A.D. *1020.*

To learn to draw a flower it is best to place a blossoming plant in a deep hollow in the ground and to look upon it. Then all its qualities may be grasped. To learn to draw a bamboo, take a branch and cast its shadow upon a white wall on a moonlight night; then its true outline can be obtained. To learn to paint a landscape, too, the method is the same. An artist should identify himself with the landscape and watch it until its significance is revealed to him.

Second, by Sir Thomas Browne in Religio Medici :

I can look for a whole day with delight upon a handsome picture, though it be but of an horse.

'Time remembered', as Swinburne pointed out, 'is grief forgotten' – a thought which was developed a stage further by Petronius when he wrote:

> Pervixi: neque enim fortuna malignior unquam
> Eripiet nobis quod prior hora dedit.

In Texts and Pretexts, *Aldous Huxley gives the following translation, which may or may not be his own:*

> I have lived; nor shall maligner fortune ever
> Take from me what an earlier hour once gave.

This couplet should be committed to memory by everybody, for use as a sort of moral first aid in moments of crisis. For me its cheering-up potential is roughly that of a double whisky-and-soda – which, alas, is all too frequently not to hand when one needs it most. Huxley goes on to contrast it with Dante's lines – which, incidentally, provide the words for the Gondolier's song in Rossini's Otello:

> Ed ella a me: Nessun maggior dolore
> Che ricordarsi del tempo felice
> Nella miseria. . . .

> Then she to me: 'There is no greater anguish
> Than to remember in black hours of sorrow
> The joyful times. . . .'

Swinburne and Petronius? Or Francesca da Rimini? Take your choice.
After the publication of the above, Frank Ashton-Gwatkin sent me his own admirable translation of the Petronius:

> I've lived it through; and nevermore
>   Can harsher fate destroy
> The glory that has gone before
>   Or afterglow of joy.

I find, too, that the same thought occurred to Thomas Moore:

> When Time, who steals our years away,
>   Shall steal our pleasures too,
> The memory of the past will stay
>   And half our joys renew.

And to Tennyson in Locksley Hall:

> This is the truth the poet sings,
> That a sorrow's crown of sorrows is remembering
> happier things.

My attention was also drawn to Alfred de Musset's passionate reply to Dante for what he called 'an insult to unhappiness':

> Dante, pourquoi dis-tu qu'il n'est pire misère
> Qu'un souvenir heureux dans les jours de douleur?
> Quel chagrin t'a dicté cette parole amère,
> Cette offense au malheur?
>
> En est-il donc moins vrai que la lumière existe,
> Et faut-il l'oublier du moment qu'il fait nuit?
> Est-ce bien, toi, grande âme immortellement triste,
> Est-ce toi qui l'as dit?
>
> Non, par ce pur flambeau dont la splendeur m'éclaire,
> Ce blasphème vanté ne vient pas de ton cœur.
> Un souvenir heureux est peut-être sur terre
> Plus vrai que le bonheur.

The interesting thing was that everbody who wrote to me seemed to agree with Petronius; but now at last Francesca has found her champion. My old friend Christopher Scaife writes from Tuscany (where, after all, people should know):

'I think that what Dante had in mind, with Francesca's words, is what Marlowe makes Mephistopheles express when he says

> Why, this is hell, nor am I out of it:
> Thinkst thou that I who saw the face of God
> And tasted the eternal joys of heaven,
> Am not tormented with ten thousand hells
> In being deprived of everlasting bliss?

'Yes, indeed: here, in this mortal life – which *must* end – recollection of happiness is as de Musset says. But in hell, whence both Francesca and Mephisto spoke, 'tis otherwise.'

COMMENT

Oh, life is a glorious cycle of song,
A medley of extemporanea;
And love is a thing that can never go wrong,
And I am Marie of Roumania.

Dorothy Parker

A Christmas Cracker

1975

I have just discovered what a pennill is. It is a traditional Welsh form of improvised verse, normally sung to a harp accompaniment. The plural is pennillion – a nice plural. This particular example, translated by Geoffrey Grigson, dates from the seventeenth century:

What happiness you gave to me
Underneath this graveyard tree
When in my embraces wound,
Dear heart, you lay above the ground.

The same thought, if somewhat differently expressed, can be found in James Thurber's glorious parody of those novels about the Deep South like Tobacco Road *or* God's Little Acre. *It is called* Bateman Comes Home *and begins:*

Old Nate Pirge sat on the rusted wreck of an ancient sewing-machine, in front of Hell Fire, which is what his shack was known as among the neighbours and to the police. He was chewing on a splinter of wood and watching the moon come up lazily out of the old cemetery in which nine of his daughters were lying, only two of whom were dead.

Here is an extract from Parson Woodforde's diary for 1778:

April 15 . . . We breakfasted, dined, supped and slept again at home. Brewed a vessel of strong Beer today. My two large Piggs, by drinking some Beer grounds taking out of one of my Barrels today, got so amazingly drunk by it, that they were not able to stand and appeared like dead things almost, and so remained all night from dinner time today. I never saw Piggs so drunk in my life. . . .

April 16 . . . My 2 Piggs are still unable to walk yet, but they are better than they were yesterday. They tumble about the yard and can by no means stand at all steady yet. In the afternoon my 2 Piggs were tolerably sober.

Love's Labour's Lost *is the first of Shakespeare's published plays to bear his name. Nobody knows quite when it was written, but most scholars seem to agree on the early 1590s. This would make it roughly contemporary with the first sonnets, and certainly none of the plays – not even* Romeo and Juliet *– shows Shakespeare more tenderly lyrical:*

> Love's feeling is more soft and sensible
> Than are the tender horns of cockled snails;
> Love's tongue proves dainty Bacchus gross in taste:
> For valour, is not Love a Hercules,
> Still climbing trees in the Hesperides?
> Subtle as Sphinx, as sweet and musical
> As bright Apollo's lute, strung with his hair;
> And when Love speaks, the voice of all the gods
> Make heaven drowsy with the harmony.

The play has a lovely, funny ending. After the famous 'When icicles hang by the wall' – ruined for me by too many reluctant recitations at school – there appears a single sentence, printed in large type in the early Quarto text,

THE WORDS OF MERCURY ARE HARSH AFTER THE SONGS OF APOLLO.

The First Folio gives this line to Don Adriano de Armado, the 'fantastical Spaniard', and has him add as an afterthought,

You that way, we this way.

There is nothing particularly profound about either of these remarks; but they provide just the sort of innocent, pointless little flourish that sends the audience away smiling.

From an old Who's Who :

SWANN, Rev. Sidney, M.A., Vicar of Lindfield, 1929–37; *b.* 30 Sept. 1862; *s.* of John Bellingham Swann, R.N.; *m.* 1st; two *s.* one *d.* 2nd, Lady Bagot (*d.* 1940). *Educ.* Marlborough; Trinity Hall, Cambridge. Rowed in the Oxford and Cambridge boat race, 1883, 1884 and 1885 (Swann junior stroked Cambridge, 1912); won Cambridge sculls and pairs, also Grand Challenge, 1886 and 1887, and Steward's, 1885 and 1887, in record times; in Japan won most things started for on land and sea; rowing, hurdling, cycling, running, pole-jumping, weight and hammer; first to cycle round Syria; rode Land's End to John O'Groats; Carlisle to London in a day; rowed home-made boat from Crosby Vicarage down the rapids of the Eden to the sea, and cut the record from England to France, 1911, rowing the Channel in 3 hours 50 minutes, faster time than anyone had ever gone between England and France by muscular power; built several flying machines, and drove motor ambulance in Belgium (1914 medal, 1915 medal, Roi de Belge Order). In 1917, when 55 years old, cycled, walked, ran, paddled, rode and swam six consecutive half-miles in 26 minutes 20 seconds, in competition with Lieut. Muller of the Danish Army; President of the National Amateur Rowing Association since 1934; *Rec :* rowing, tennis, cycling, motoring. *Address :* Lindfield, Hayward's Heath, Sussex.

He died on 3 August 1942. Humility was clearly not his forte but I wonder whether muscular Christianity has ever been carried further. Probably not ; but the story of Mr Swann has. Some time after the entry above was published in the 1975 Cracker, *I received a letter from Mrs Marjorie Crossley of Shottisham, Suffolk. With Mrs Crossley's permission, I reproduce it here in full :*

By 1937 the Rev. Sidney Swann had become very eccentric, and was persuaded to retire. The living was given to the Rev. Daunton Fear. Mr Swann continued to live in the Bowery, two fourteenth-century cottages he had converted into a house, almost opposite the church on Lindfield Street.

He was put in a mental home a year or so later.

It was in the spring of 1939 that we hired the Bowery from the Master of Lunacy (?) on a five-year lease. The furniture had all been removed, but on a wall in the dining-room there still hung a number of tasselled caps, and sculls painted with college colours, etc.

It was a splendid old house with a king-post, panelling, etc., and we felt privileged to live there, but the village seethed with stories of Mr Swann's uncontrolled behaviour, ruthlessness and his final removal in a strait-jacket.

The climax had come when, deciding to do away with Lady Bagot (she never called herself Mrs Swann), he went up to London and bought a large cook's knife. The house had two staircases with heavy oak doors at the top; he went up, shooting the bolts behind him. The two maids fled in terror to Mr Fear, who got a ladder and entered the bedroom through the window on the street. He saved Lady Bagot. Swann was overcome and taken away, swearing to avenge himself on Fear. (That sounds an unlikely name, but is correct though possibly spelt wrongly.)

One day, returning from war-work, I saw a taxi outside my door. I entered from the garden, heard the bell and opened the front door. A very large man walked in past me to the sitting-room, sat down and said, 'I am Mr Swann. I have escaped from the asylum and I want my house back.'

I thought in the circumstances it was best not to argue, so I agreed, only pleading a little time to get alternative accommodation. He seemed satisfied and went. I found out afterwards that the news spread round the village that 'Mr Swann was back!', and some tradesmen, including the butcher with his cleaver, were in an upstairs window in the Tiger opposite in case there was any rough stuff!

He remained hidden in his sister's house in the village, and when he felt safe from re-certification he took lodgings down the street, and prowled about the garden at night, which the children did not care for. After three or four weeks my husband joined the R.A.F. again and I took the children up north. As our furniture went out of the front his came in at the back. Lady Bagot having died, he remarried and finally died after a fall from his bicycle.

Mrs Fear became ill with worry for the life of her husband, so they gave up the living and I heard of him last at Gravesend.

We still have two beautiful panels of wrought iron which we found in the garage and bought before we heard that he had wrenched them out of a church in Surrey.

Of Lady Bagot, Grizel Hartley writes:

The first time she received Holy Communion from her husband, she drained the wine to the dregs and said 'Perfectly delicious!' and handed it back. (This, from Sidney Swann's son, the one who was the chaplain of Trinity Hall, Cambridge, who told it to Hubert.)

My daughter Artemis found the following passage in the Journal *of George Fox, founder of the Quakers. I should like to have transcribed it in the original orthography, but Fox's spelling and punctuation are one degree too eccentric, even for the year 1651.*

And as I was one time walking in a Close with several friends I lift up my head and I espied three steeple-house spires and they struck at my life; and I asked friends what they was and they said Lichfield; and so the word of the Lord came to me, thither I might go; and I bid the friends that was with me walk into the house from me, and they did; and as soon as they was gone – for I said nothing to them – but I went over hedge and ditch till I came within a mile of Lichfield. And when I came into a great field where there was shepherds keeping their sheep I was commanded of the Lord to put off my shoes of a sudden; and I stood still, and the word of the Lord was like a fire in me; and being winter I untied my shoes and put them off. . . .

And the poor shepherds trembled, and were astonished; and so I went about a mile until I came into the town, and as soon as I came within the town the word of the Lord came unto me again to cry 'Woe unto the bloody city of Lichfield'; so I went up and down the streets crying 'Woe unto the bloody city of Lichfield', and being market day I went into the market place and went up and down in several places of it and made stands crying 'Woe unto the bloody city of Lichfield' and no one touched me or laid hands of me. . . .

And so at last I came to a ditch and washed my feet and put on my shoes; and when I had done I considered why I should go and cry against that city and call it that bloody city: though the Parliament had the Minster one while and the King another while and much blood had been shed in the town, yet that could not be charged upon the town. But as I went down the town there run like a channel of blood down the streets, and the market place was like a pool of blood. This I saw as I went through it crying Woe to the bloody city of Lichfield.

But after I came to see that there was 1000 martyrs in Diocletian's time was martyred in Lichfield; and so I must go in my stockings through the channel of their blood and come into the pool of their blood in their market place.

There is a painting of this extraordinary scene in the Public Library at Lichfield. Macaulay said of Fox that he was 'too much disordered for liberty, and not sufficiently disordered for Bedlam'.

Victor Hugo remembers the first stirrings of adolescence :

J'allais au Luxembourg rêver, ô temps lointain,
Dès l'aurore, et j'étais moi-même le matin.
Les nids dialoguaient tout bas, et les allées
Désertes étaient d'ombre et de soleil mêlées;
J'étais pensif, j'étais profond, j'étais niais.
Comme je regardais et comme j'épiais!
Qui? La Vénus, l'Hébé, la nymphe chasseresse.
Je sentais du printemps l'invisible caresse.
Je guettais l'inconnu. J'errais. Quel curieux
Que Chérubin en qui s'éveille Des Grieux!
O femme! mystère! être ignoré qu'on encense!
Parfois j'étais obscène à force d'innocence.
Mon regard violait la vague nudité
Des déesses, debout sous les feuilles d'été;
Je contemplais de loin ces rondeurs peu vêtues,
Et j'étais amoureux de toutes les statues;
Et j'en ai mis plus d'une en colère, je crois.
Les audaces dans l'ombre égalent les effrois,
Et, hardi comme un page et tremblant comme un lièvre,
Oubliant latin, grec, algèbre, ayant la fièvre
Qui résiste aux Bezouts et brave les Restauts,*
Je restais là stupide au bas des piédestaux,
Comme si j'attendais que le vent sous quelque arbre
Soulevât les jupons d'une Diane en marbre.

*Bezout, Etienne, author of *Cours complet de mathématiques,* 1780. Restaut,
Pierre, author of *Principes généraux et raisonnés de la grammaire française,* 1730.

Once, long ago, a lady said to me 'You see, I'm afraid I have rather a sense of humour.' It struck me at the time as perhaps the most nauseating sentence I had ever heard pronounced; I was all the more delighted, some years later, to find the following passage in Dean Swift's 'Hints towards an Essay on Conversation':

> Others make a vanity of telling their faults; they are the strangest men in the world; they cannot dissemble; they own it is a folly; they have lost abundance of advantages by it; but, if you would give them the world, they cannot help it; there is something in their nature that abhors insincerity and constraint; with many other insufferable topics of the same altitude.

One of the minor surprises in literature is Lewis Carroll's strangely unseason-
able and petulant preface to the Christmas 1896 reprint (Sixty-first Thou-
sand) of Through the Looking-Glass. *It ends:*

I take this opportunity of announcing that the Nursery 'Alice', hitherto priced at four shillings, net, is now to be had on the same terms as the ordinary shilling picture-books – although I feel sure that it is, in every quality (except the *text* itself, on which I am not qualified to pronounce), greatly superior to them. Four shillings was a perfectly reasonable price to charge, considering the very heavy initial outlay I had incurred: still, as the Public have prac-tically said 'We will *not* give more than a shilling for a picture-book, however artistically got-up,' I am content to reckon my outlay on the book as so much dead loss, and, rather than let the little ones, for whom it was written, go without it, I am selling it at a price which is, to me, much the same thing as *giving* it away.

Resignedly beneath the sky
The melancholy waters lie.
So blend the turrets and shadows there,
That all seem pendulous in air,
While from a proud tower in the town
Death looks gigantically down.

Poe, *The City and the Sea*

When Death came at last to Poe, hardly anybody seemed to notice. It was twenty-six years before his grave was given a tombstone, and even then only one American writer attended the ceremony – Walt Whitman.

Book dedications provide a fertile field for commonplace collectors. One of my favourites is that of Colonel Angus Buchanan's book on the Sahara, published half a century ago. It reads:

To Feri n'Gashi,
Only a Camel
But steel-true and great of heart.

Col. Buchanan is, however, run close by Mrs Frances Simpson, who thus dedicates her book Cats for Pleasure and Profit:

To the many kind friends, known and
unknown, that I have made
in Pussydom.

To my farther great benefit, as I grew older, I thus saw nearly all the noblemen's houses in England; in reverent and healthy delight of uncovetous admiration, – perceiving as soon as I could perceive any political truth at all, that it was probably much happier to live in a small house, and have Warwick Castle to be astonished at, than to live in Warwick Castle and have nothing to be astonished at; but that, at all events, it would not make Brunswick Square in the least more pleasantly habitable, to pull Warwick Castle down. And at this day, though I have kind invitations enough to visit America, I could not, even for a couple of months, live in a country so miserable as to possess no castles.

Ruskin, Praeterita

Goethe, on the other hand, took precisely the opposite line :

Amerika, du hast es besser
Als unser Kontinent, der alte,
Hast keine verfallenen Schlösser
Und keine Basalte.

But Thomas Hardy was, predictably, on Ruskin's side. Here is the first verse from his 'On an Invitation to the United States' :

My ardours for surprize nigh lost
Since Life has bared its bones to me,
I shrink to seek a modern coast
Whose riper times have yet to be;
Where the new regions claim them free
From that long drip of human tears
Which peoples old in tragedy
Have left upon the centuried years.

John Wesley on how to bring up children :

Break their wills betimes; begin this great work before they can run alone, before they can speak plain or perhaps speak at all. Let him have nothing he cries for, absolutely nothing, great or small. Make him do as he is bid, if you whip him ten times running to effect it. Break his will now and his soul will live and he will probably bless you to all eternity.

I wonder.

This compares interestingly with the advice given by another rather different divine, St Bernardino of Siena, on the correct treatment of a servant girl :

If you do not accustom her to doing all the work she will become a lazy little lump of flesh. Do not allow her any leisure, I tell you. Only if you keep her fully occupied will you prevent her wasting time looking out of the window.

In the Cracker *for 1972 I included two stories about Mrs Siddons. That might be thought enough; but Benjamin Robert Haydon's account of one of her evening parties has proved impossible to resist.*

She acts Macbeth herself better than either Kemble or Kean. It is extraordinary the awe this wonderful woman inspires. After her first reading the men retired to tea. While we were all eating toast and tingling cups and saucers, she began again. It was like the effect of a mass bell at Madrid. All noise ceased; we slunk to our seats like boors, two or three of the most distinguished men of the day, with the very toast in their mouths, afraid to bite. It was curious to see Lawrence in this predicament, to hear him bite by degrees, and then stop for fear of making too much crackle, his eyes full of water from the constraint; and at the same time to hear Mrs Siddons' 'eye of newt and toe of frog!' and then to see Lawrence give a sly bite, and then look awed and pretend to be listening. I went away highly gratified, and as I stood on the landing-place to get cool I overheard my own servant in the hall say: 'What! is that the old lady making such a noise?' 'Yes.' 'Why, she makes as much noise as ever!' 'Yes,' was the answer; 'she tunes her pipes as well as ever she did.'

I must not omit a foolish singularity, in relation to the women dancers at *Naples*, that, in consequence of an order from court, in the late King's time, they all wear black drawers. I presume it was from some conceit on the subject of modesty, but it appears very odd and ridiculous. I shall not enter into any detail of the two houses; but their dresses, their scenery, and their actors, are much more despicable than one could possibly imagine.

Samuel Sharp,
Letters from Italy, 1767

In The Sun King, *Nancy Mitford gives an unforgettable portrait of Louis XIV's queen, Marie-Thérèse of Spain:*

If her husband had no reason to be proud of her he had no reason to be ashamed either. But she had the mentality of a child, liked to play with little dogs and half-mad dwarfs and never learnt to speak French properly; she made no impact on her subjects. In spite of a pretty face she was not attractive; she had short legs and black teeth from eating too much chocolate and garlic. The King was fond of her and treated her in a fatherly way; and she worshipped him, though she avoided being left alone with him, it embarrassed her. One kind look from him made her happy all day. . . .

He made love with her at least twice a month. Everybody knew when this had happened because she went to Communion the next day. She also liked to be teased about it, and would rub her little hands and wink with her large blue eyes.

When Marie-Thérèse died, Louis is said to have murmured: 'C'est le premier déplaisir qu'elle m'ait fait.' Compare Pope's epitaph on the young Simon Harcourt:

To this sad shrine, whoe'er thou art, draw near;
Here lies the friend most loved, the son most dear:
Who ne'er knew joy but friendship might divide,
Or gave his father grief but when he died.

ANSWER TO CHLOE JEALOUS

Dear Chloe, how blubbered is that pretty face!
Thy cheek all on fire, and thy hair all uncurled.
Prithee, quit this caprice; and (as old Falstaff says)
Let us e'en talk a little like folks of this world.

How canst thou presume thou hast leave to destroy
The beauties which Venus but lent to thy keeping?
Those looks were designed to inspire love and joy:
More ordinary eyes may serve people for weeping.

To be vexed at a trifle or two that I writ
Your judgment at once and my passion you wrong:
You take that for fact which will scarce be found wit,
'Od's life! must one swear to the truth of a song?

What I speak, my fair Chloe, and what I write, shows
The difference there is betwixt Nature and Art:
I court others in verse, but love thee in prose:
And they have my whimsies, but thou hast my heart.

The God of us verse-men, you know, child, the sun
How after his journeys he sets up his rest:
If at morning o'er Earth 'tis his fancy to run,
At night he reclines on his Thetis's breast.

So when I am wearied with wandering all day,
To thee, my delight, in the evening I come;
No matter what beauties I saw in my way,
They were but my visits, but thou art my home.

Then finish, dear Chloe, this pastoral war,
And let us like Horace and Lydia agree:
For thou art a girl as much brighter than her
As he was a poet sublimer than me.

                                        Matthew Prior

Bamber Gascoigne has introduced me to this account of the death of Robert Henryson, the Scottish poet. He died in about 1506. What follows was recorded in 1635 by Sir Francis Kynaston in his manuscript edition of Chaucer, so cannot be considered first-hand testimony; but if it is not true, it should be.

This Mr Robert Henryson he was questionles a learned and witty man, and it is pitty we have no more of his works, because being very old he dyed of a diarrhoea or fluxe, of whom there goes this merry, though somewhat unsavoury tale, that all physitians having given him over and he lying drawing his last breath there came an old woman unto him, who was held a witch, and asked him whether he would be cured, to whom he sayed very willingly, then quod she there is a whikey tree in the lower end of your orchard, and if you will go and walk but thrice about it, and thrice repeat theis wordes whikey tree whikey tree take away this fluxe from me you shall be presently cured, he told her that beside he was extreme faint and weake it was extreme frost and snow and that it was impossible for him to go: she told him that unles he did so it was impossible he should recover. Mr Henrysoun then lifting up himselfe, and pointing to an oaken table that was in the roome, asked her and said gude dame I pray ye tell me, if it would not do as well if I repeated thrice theis words oken burd oken burd garre me shit a hard turde. The woman seeing herself derided and scorned ran out of the house in a great passion and Mr Henrysoun within a halfe a quarter of an houre departed this life.

EPITAPH FOR HIMSELF

Ci-gît celui qui t'aimait trop
Pour ton bonheur et son repos.

Hilaire Belloc

Gilbert White, author of The Natural History and Antiquities of Selborne, *kept his journal for a quarter of a century, from 1768 to 1793 when he died. No literary work has ever recorded more precisely, more sensitively and yet with less pretension, the changing face of the countryside with the passing of the seasons. Most of the individual items are in themselves unmemorable – it is the cumulative effect that counts – but occasionally we are pulled up short :*

4 December 1770 :
Most owls seem to hoot exactly in B flat according to several pitch-pipes used in tuning of harpsichords, and as strictly at concert pitch.

8 February 1782 :
Venus *shadows* very strongly, showing the bars of the windows on the floors and walls.

The first of these entries brought a most serendipitous contribution from Antony Head, quoting Professor Howard Evans of Fort Collins, Colorado :

Even the simple wing sounds of midges and mosquitoes play a role in bringing the sexes together. In this case it is the female that attracts the male by the hum of her wings, a fact quickly apparent to singers who hit a G in the vicinity of a swarm and end up with a mouthful of male mosquitoes.

What, then, is the secret of Voltaire's greatness? In the first place, his supremely acute and active intelligence, his insatiable curiosity. In the second place, his energy, his activity. He had the courage and the restlessness of a fly, and the sting of a wasp. His style reflects all his faults and all his qualities. It is neither eloquent, nor poetical, nor coloured; he has not the imagination which transmutes sensations and impressions by the alchemy of art into a mysterious metal. He sees everything from the point of view of reason, in black and white; there exist for him certain things which are true, and certain things which are false and therefore foolish, folly. Follies must be remedied, or killed by ridicule; that is to say, by reason. In this he is 'French of the French' and lord of human sneers. He was, and always remained, more than a spoilt child, a naughty boy. He was a disintegrator. He nibbled like a tireless mouse with formidable corrosive teeth at the pillars of Society and the old régime, and left them, shaking and rotten, for the Revolution to pull down.

If it is true, as a Frenchman once said, that '*la France n'est pas gouvernable*', Voltaire is in part to blame. Nobody ever more successfully undermined the prestige of all possible government. He undermined the faith of the *bourgeoisie* in two things – government and religion. His philosophy was entirely practical. He was temperamentally irreligious and disrespectful; he preached disbelief, not only by precept, but by example; he made disrespect easy and popular; he taught the *bourgeoisie* and the half-educated not only how to do without religion, but how to laugh at it, how to treat it as something absurd. His god was a philosophical axiom acceptable to the reason; far more than Peter the Great, he was the first Bolshevist. His fundamental ideas and his philosophy are based on the all-importance of material welfare and progress. According to Mermilod, the cry of the masses is: '*Vous m'avez ôté l'espérance du ciel, et la crainte de l'enfer; il ne me reste que la terre: je l'aurai.*'

The cry might have been addressed to Voltaire.

From *French Literature*, by Maurice Baring

With that reference to the 'spoilt child', was Baring, I wonder, subconsciously remembering the epitaph suggested for Voltaire by an anonymous 'Lady of Lausanne'?

Ci-gît l'enfant gâté du monde qu'il gâta.

The late Sir Compton Mackenzie, invited to name the ten most beautiful
words in the English language, ran them into blank verse:

Carnation, azure, peril, moon, forlorn,
Heart, silence, shadow, April, apricot.

A good selection, which I prefer to his second team:

Damask and damson, doom and harlequin and fire,
Autumn, vanity, flame, nectarine, desire.

My Life and Times, Octave Seven

Here, from Peter Fleming's The Siege at Peking, *is an account of the tribulations suffered by the foreign residents of the city during the Boxer rebellion in 1900.*

Although some of the non-combatants had plenty of leisure, the besieged had few recreations. After Kierulff's store was looted (by permission of its proprietor, who thought it was going to fall into Chinese hands) a number of gramophones and musical boxes added to the almost perpetual din. In the evenings the American missionaries gathered outside the door of the chapel in which some eighty of them were quartered and sang 'Marching Through Georgia', 'Nearer, my God, to Thee', 'De Ringtailed Coon' and other melodies. Sometimes a Russian lady of striking beauty, who had been an opera-singer, obliged with an *aria* as the nocturnal volleys whistled overhead. The well-stocked library of Mr Cockburn, the First Secretary, provided some with solace. It included several books dealing with the Indian Mutiny, and accounts of the Relief of Lucknow were in keen demand; the fate of Cawnpore was less closely studied.

My beloved spake, and said unto me, Rise up, my love, my fair one, and come away.

For lo, the winter is past, the rain is over and gone;

The flowers appear on the earth; the time of the singing of birds is come, and the voice of the turtle is heard in our land;

The fig tree putteth forth her green figs, and the vines with the tender grape give a good smell. Arise my love, my fair one, and come away.

O my dove, that art in the clefts of the rock, in the secret places of the stairs, let me see thy countenance, let me hear thy voice; for sweet is thy voice, and thy countenance is comely.

Take us the foxes, the little foxes, that spoil the vines: for our vines have tender grapes.

My beloved is mine, and I am his: he feedeth among the lilies.

The Song of Solomon, 2:9

A
Christmas
Cracker

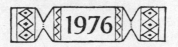

How deep is my decay! It is long since I saw the Duke of Chou in a dream.

Confucius

It is refreshing to note in Sir Thomas Malory's Morte d'Arthur *that the standards of chivalry prevailing at the Round Table were not – even if we leave aside the lamentable lapses of Sir Lancelot – of a uniformly high order. Even King Arthur himself seems to have slipped a little at times:*

Ryght so com in the lady, on a whyght palfery, and cryed alowde unto kynge Arthur and sayde, 'Sir, suffir me not to have thys despite, for the brachet* ys myne that the knyght hath ladde away.'

'I may nat do therewith,' seyde the kynge.

So with thys there com a knyght rydying all armed on a grete horse, and toke the lady away wyth forse wyth hym, and ever she cryed and made grete dole. So when she was gone the kynge was gladde, for she made such a noyse.

*a female hound.

A never-failing delight is the diary of William Allingham. He seems to have been a friend of virtually all the leading writers and painters of mid-nineteenth-century England, and to have acted in some degree as a Boswell to everybody – particularly to Tennyson, whom he worshipped. The first time he went to call, Frederick Tennyson – the poet's eldest brother – and Edward Fitzgerald were of the company.

Mr Fitzgerald stood up for Pope's 'Homer', and tried in vain to get T.'s approval.

'You think it very wonderful, surely?'

T. – 'I don't think I do.'

'Oh yes you do, Alfred!'

T. – 'No, I do not.'

Frederick T. set Schiller above Goethe, to which I strongly objected. A.T. said: 'If one of you is for Goethe, and the other for Schiller, you'll never agree on poetry.' Moore was mentioned; his skilful versification in fitting words to music. T. objected to the line

'She is far from the land where her young hero sleeps.'

I did not find much the matter with it, but T. would not allow 'young hero' to pass, the metre requiring a dactyl there: 'I wonder you don't see,' he said. 'Subaltern' I suggested. 'Yes, that would do, as far as sound goes.' . . .

I spilt some port on the cloth, and T., with his usual imperturbability, spread salt on it, remarking as he did so, 'I believe it never comes out!' Then we went upstairs to tea.

Two anecdotes of the French Revolution, recounted by Horace Walpole to Hannah More.

Did you hear of Madame Elizabeth, the King's sister? a saint like yourself. She doted on her brother, for she certainly knew his soul. In the tumult in July, hearing the populace and the *poissardes* had broken into the palace, she flew to the King, and by embracing him tried to shield his person. The populace took her for the Queen, cried out *'Voilà cette chienne, cette Autrichienne!'* and were proceeding to violence. Somebody, to save her, screamed *'Ce n'est pas la Reine, c'est –.'* The Princess said *'Ah! mon Dieu! ne les détrompez pas.'* If that was not the most sublime instance of perfect innocence ready prepared for death, I know not where to find one. Sublime indeed, too, was the sentence of good father Edgeworth, the King's confessor, who, thinking his royal penitent a little dismayed just before the fatal stroke, cried out, *'Montez, digne fils de St Louis! Le ciel vous est ouvert.'* The holy martyr's countenance brightened up, and he submitted at once.

... I do love these ancient ruins:
We never tread upon them but we set
Our foot upon some reverend history:
And, questionless, here in this open court,
Which now lies naked to the injuries
Of stormy weather, some men lie interred
Loved the church so well, and gave so largely to 't,
They thought it should have canopied their bones
Till doomsday. But all things have their end.
Churches and cities, which have diseases like to men,
Must have like death that we have.

> John Webster,
> *The Duchess of Malfi*

Clive Barnes, reviewing a performance of the play in Stratford, Ontario, some years ago, wrote of

Webster's poetry sputtering but gloriously, like smoky candles at a black mass.

Evil isn't an army that besieges a city from outside the walls. It is a native of the city. It is the mutiny of the garrison, the poison in the water, the ashes in the bread.

Charles Morgan

Less than a month after Waterloo, Napoleon – now on the run – arrived at Rochefort. There he addressed this letter to the Prince Regent. The original, handed to Captain Frederick Maitland, R.N., commanding officer of H.M.S. Bellerophon, is now in the Royal Archives at Windsor.

Rochefort, 13 juillet, 1815

Altesse Royale,

En butte aux factions qui divisent mon pays, et à l'inimitié des plus grandes puissances de l'Europe, j'ai consommé ma carrière politique. Je viens, comme Thémistocle, m'asseoir sur le foyer du peuple britannique; je me mets sous la protection de ses lois, que je réclame de Votre Altesse Royale, comme celle du plus puissant, du plus constant, du plus généreux de mes ennemis.

Napoléon.

What a magnificent letter it is; proud, courteous, tragic and brief – with a note of genuine poetry and a resonance that continues long after one has finished reading it. And how sad that the Prince Regent did not think it worthy of a reply.

Christopher Hibbert writes to point out that 'it was on the government's advice and with the agreement of the other Allied powers that Napoleon's request was not granted. The Regent declared approvingly: "Upon my word, a very proper letter: much more so, I must say, than any I ever received from Louis XVIII."'

Of all the developments that we saw on the world stage in 1976, none was more tragic than the virtual destruction of the city of Beirut. James Morris wrote a beautiful essay on it in its prime, ending like this:

Nowhere can you find a combination more breath-taking of sea and snow, age and vigour, history and persiflage. Only at the Levantine end of the Mediterranean could a Beirut exist, with all these undertones of antiquity, graft and tolerance. Is she really a great city, this wayward paragon? Scarcely, by the standards of Berlin or San Francisco, Tokyo or Moscow; but she is great in a different kind. She is great like a voluptuous courtesan, a shady merchant-prince, the scent of jasmine or the flash of a dazzling scandal. She has scarcely achieved greatness, nor even had it thrust upon her: but greatness has often spent a night in her arms, and a little lingers.

Cities

> Ill fares the land, to hast'ning ills a prey,
> Where wealth accumulates and men decay.

So, truthfully if unmusically, wrote Oliver Goldsmith. But I find that I have still more sympathy with Hilaire Belloc's rejoinder:

> But how much more unfortunate are those
> Where wealth decays and population grows.

Freya Stark describes, in The Lycian Shore, *a visit to Cnidus, in Asia Minor:*

As I came down from the causeway through the theatre, a black snake like a shy god slid into the laurel thicket; I stepped over the stones rattled by earthquakes on their foundations, and climbed from terrace to terrace of corn where the peasants build shallow walls round the pockets of the ancient houses. The full ears, ready for the harvest, beat their slight weight against my passing hand, as if they too would spend their weak resistance for the headland's warm and living peace. So remote, so undisturbed was the great hollow, that its own particular divinity seemed to fill it – complete in being as a cup is filled to its brim. There was no judgment here, but only consequence of actions; the good corn filled itself out in deeper places and the bad dwindled among stones, and all things were a part of each other in a soil that someone's building two thousand or more years ago had fattened or spoiled. A fair-haired woman, still beautiful, with green eyes, was reaping. I asked if I might photograph, and she called her husband, who came climbing up and stood beside her, and glanced at her and smiled when I said she was like the English to look at: they were both pleased by her fairness, and there was a happy friendliness between them. He had the oval face of the Mediterranean, and she the straight northern brows: and the history of the world had washed over Cnidus to produce them both, from the days when their ancestors, in the oldest city of the peninsula, joined in building the Hellenium in Egypt, or sent the first caryatid to Delphi.

For a hundred years or more, upset British stomachs used to be soothed by that magnificent patent medicine whose full name was 'Dr J. Collis Browne's (MRCSL, Ex-Army Medical Staff) CHLORODYNE'. The leaflet enclosed with each bottle of Chlorodyne was a treat in itself. It began:

This well-known preparation was realized in 1848, while Dr Collis Browne was serving with the Indian Army, but was not introduced for public use until after prolonged trials it was proved to possess valuable remedial properties.

The medical properties of Chlorodyne are – ANODYNE, DIAPHORETIC, SEDATIVE, ASTRINGENT, ANTI-SPASMODIC. It is agreeable to taste and has a soothing and pleasant effect on the patient.

Its effects are characterized by the following phases: –

1st – A few moments after taking the Chlorodyne, a gentle heat is experienced at the stomach, succeeded by a general glow and relief from pain.

2nd – A tranquil, composed state gradually takes place, with or without sleep.

3rd – A comfortable and regular sleep of normal duration ensues, *during which a favourable change takes place.*

Overleaf we find testimonials, among them the following:

From W. VESALIUS PETTIGREW, MD, Hon.FRCS, England:

I have no hesitation in stating, after a fair trial of Chlorodyne, that I have never met with any medicine so efficacious as an Anti-Spasmodic and Sedative. I have used it in Diarrhoea, and other diseases, and am most perfectly satisfied with the results.

EDWARD WHYMPER, Esq., the celebrated Mountaineer, writes on February 16th, 1896: –

I always carry Dr J. Collis Browne's Chlorodyne with me on my travels, and have used it effectively *on others* on Mont Blanc.

From CASSEL'S HISTORY OF THE BOER WAR, page 542: –

'Gaunter and gaunter grew the soldiers of the Queen. Hunger and sickness played havoc with those fine regiments. But somehow the RAMC managed to patch the men up with Chlorodyne and quinine.'

The italics are my own.

When this appeared in the 1976 Cracker, *I was rewarded by a letter from Lord Amulree, who wrote:*

'About five years ago I assisted a friend of mine in a search for Dr Collis Browne's house at Ramsgate: we had difficulty in finding it because, after his death, it had become for a short time a house of ill fame and the subsequent owner had the name changed. Messrs Davenport, the firm that makes Chlorodyne, were interested, and they paid to have a memorial plaque put on the house. This was unveiled by the Mayor of Ramsgate: then we had a lunch at the green Pugin hotel on the front, which is just next door to the road where the Collis Browne house is. . . . We also identified Collis Browne's grave in the overgrown churchyard, and that too has been tidied up by Davenport's.'

At about the same time I also quoted the testimonials in a radio broadcast, and received a very nice letter from the Managing Director of J. T. Davenport, Ltd, enclosing a beautiful coloured brochure about the life and work of Dr Collis Browne, from which I learnt that his interest was not confined to pharmaceuticals: he also invented a sort of marine propeller. Poor Davenport's – they have been hit twice in ten years by drugs legislation, the first reducing the permitted chloroform content from 14 to 5 per cent, the second the morphine content from 0.14 per cent to 0.02 per cent; with each blow the name was changed, from 'Chlorodyne' to 'compound' and finally to 'mixture'. But the name of J. Collis Browne remains inviolate on every bottle and I am assured that, as the morphine content of the dose has remained the same, the preparation is as effective as ever it was.

Pour l'enfant amoureux de contes et d'estampes,
L'univers est égal à son vaste appétit.
Ah, que le monde est grand à la clarté des lampes!
Aux yeux du souvenir que le monde est petit!

Baudelaire

Or, as Jules Laforgue put it,

Dieu! Que la vie est quotidienne!

The Rev. Sydney Smith, like Gibbon, Oscar Wilde, Pepys, Dr Johnson and epitaphs, tends to overload commonplace books if the compiler exercises anything less than the steeliest self-control. Some of his remarks, as when he told the child stroking a tortoise that it might as well stroke the dome of St Paul's to please the Dean and Chapter, or compared heaven to the eating of pâté de foie gras *to the sound of trumpets, are anyway so well-known as to be almost hackneyed. But others are less familiar :*

I must believe in the Apostolic Succession, there being no other way of accounting for the descent of the Bishop of Exeter from Judas Iscariot.

Similarly, his description of Lord John Russell :

There is no better man in England than Lord John Russell; but his worst failure is that he is utterly ignorant of all moral fear; there is nothing he would not undertake. I believe he would perform the operation for the stone – build St Peter's – or assume (with or without ten minutes' notice) the command of the Channel Fleet; and no one would discover by his manner that the patient had died – the Church tumbled down – and the Channel Fleet been knocked to atoms.

Indeed, what reason may not go to school to the wisdom of bees, ants and spiders? What wise hand teacheth them to do what reason cannot teach us? Ruder hands stand amazed at those prodigious pieces of nature, whales, elephants, dromedaries, and camels; these, I confess, are the colossuses and majestic pieces of her hand; but in these narrow engines there is more curious mathematics; and the civility of these little citizens more neatly sets forth the wisdom of their Maker.

Sir Thomas Browne,
Religio Medici

Quotations in Icelandic have tended to be rather the exception than the rule in Crackers; *but I find it impossible to resist the temptation to include the following example, quoted by W. H. Auden in* Letters from Iceland, *of an Icelandic lullaby:*

Sofúr thu svid thitt
Svartur i áugum
Far i fulan pytt
Fullan af dráugum.

It means:

Sleep, you black-eyed pig.
Fall into a deep pit full of ghosts.

There are two Old Wives' Tales in English literature. One, as everybody knows, is by Arnold Bennett; the other is by the Elizabethan playwright George Peele. It is a satire – and not, so far as I can judge, a very good one; revivals are unlikely. But it contains two unselfconscious little lyrics that seem to me to touch the heights of pure poetry.

A head comes up with eares of Corne, and she combes them into her lap.

Faire maiden white and red,
Combe me smoothe, and stroke my head:
And thou shalt have some cockell bread.
Gently dippe, but not too deepe,
For feare thou make the goulden beard to weep.
Faire maide, white and redde,
Combe me smooth, and stroke my head;
And every haire a sheave shall be,
And every sheave a goulden tree.

When as the Rie reach to the chin,
And chopcherrie chopcherrie ripe within,
Strawberries swimming in the creame,
And schoole boyes playing in the streame;
Then O, then O, then O my true love said,
Till that time come againe,
Shee could not live a maid.

For an interesting postscript on cockell bread, John Yeoman drew my attention to John Aubrey (Lansdowne MS, N₀. 231):

Young wenches have a wanton sport which they call moulding of Cockle-bread, viz. they get up on a table-board, and then gather up their knees and their coates with their hands as high as they can, and then they wabble to and fro, as if they were kneading of dowgh, and say these words, viz.

My dame is sick and gone to bed,
And I'le go mould my Cockle-bread.

I did imagine nothing to have been in this but meer wantonnesse of youth. But I find in Burchardus, in his 'Methodus Confitendi' . . . one of the Articles (on the VII. Commandment) of interrogating a young woman is, 'If she did ever, "subigere panem clunibus", and then bake it, and give it to one she loved to eate, "ut in majorem modum exardesceret amor".' So here I find it to be a relique of naturall magick – an unlawful philtrum.

Man is so intelligent that he feels impelled to invent theories to account for what happens in the world. Unfortunately, he is not quite intelligent enough, in most cases, to find correct explanations. So that when he acts on his theories, he behaves very often like a lunatic. Thus, no animal is clever enough, when there is a drought, to imagine that the rain is being withheld by evil spirits, or as a punishment for its transgressions. Therefore you never see animals going through the absurd and often horrible fooleries of magic and religion. No horse, for example, would kill one of its foals in order to make the wind change its direction. Dogs do not ritually urinate in the hope of persuading heaven to do the same and send down rain. Asses do not bray a liturgy to cloudless skies. Nor do cats attempt, by abstinence from cats' meat, to wheedle the feline spirits into benevolence. Only man behaves with such gratuitous folly. It is the price he has to pay for being intelligent, but not, as yet, quite intelligent enough.

Aldous Huxley,
Texts and Pretexts

Therefore all seasons shall be sweet to thee,
Whether the summer clothe the general earth
With greenness, or the redbreast sit and sing
Betwixt the tufts of snow on the bare branch
Of mossy apple-tree, while the nigh thatch
Smokes in the sun-thaw; whether the eave-drops fall
Heard only in the trances of the blast,
Or if the secret ministry of frost
Shall hang them up in silent icicles,
Quietly shining to the quiet moon.
                              Coleridge

There is a memorial in the graveyard of Saddleworth church, Yorkshire, on which, in letters carved nearly an inch deep, is inscribed :

HERE LIE INTERRED THE DREADFULLY
BRUISED AND LACERATED BODIES OF
WILLIAM BRADBURY AND HIS SON THOMAS
BOTH OF GREENFIELD WHO WERE TOGETHER
SAVAGELY MURDERED IN AN UNUSUALLY
HORRID MANNER ON MONDAY NIGHT, APRIL
2 1832.

. . . .

Such interest did their tragic end excite
That ere they were removed from human sight
Thousands on thousands daily came to see
The bloody scene of the catastrophe.

Tant que mes yeus pourront larmes espandre,
A l'heur passé avec toy regretter;
Et qu'aus sanglots et soupirs resister
Pourra ma voix, et un peu faire entendre;

Tant que ma main pourra les cordes tendre
Du mignart lut, pour tes graces chanter;
Tant que l'esprit se voudra contenter
De ne vouloir rien fors que toy comprendre;

Je ne souhaitte encore point mourir:
Mais, quand mes yeus je sentiray tarir,
Ma voix cassée, et ma main impuissante,

Et mon esprit, en ce mortel séjour,
Ne pouvant plus montrer signe d'amante;
Priray la Mort noircir mon plus cler jour.

This sonnet, by Louise Labé, who lived from 1525 to 1565 – like pretty Polly Oliver, she went to the wars dressed up as a man – has always seemed to me one of the most beautiful in the French language. Some years ago I tried, not very successfully, to translate it:

While I have tears that start into my eyes
At memories of joys that we have known;
And while my voice, still master of its own,
Is not yet choked with sobbing and with sighs;

While still my hand has cunning, to devise
A lover's cadence to the lute's soft tone,
And while, in understanding you alone,
I no more wisdom need to make me wise;

How could I wish, as yet, that I were dead?
But when these eyes have no more tears to shed,
This voice has cracked, these hands have lost their art,

And when no longer can this earthbound heart
Declare itself a lover – then I'll pray
For Death to blacken out my brightest day.

If you cannot read all your books, at any rate handle, or as it were, fondle them – peer into them, let them fall open where they will, read from the first sentence that arrests the eye, set them back on the shelves with your own hands, arrange them on your own plan so that if you do not know what is in them, you at least know where they are. Let them be your friends; let them at any rate be your acquaintances. If they cannot enter the circle of your life, do not deny them at least a nod of recognition.

Winston S. Churchill,
Painting as a Pastime

From Mr Brian Porter of Aberystwyth University comes this little-known account of the marriage of Mrs Jacqueline Kennedy and Mr Aristotle Onassis, clearly dictated by the shade of Edward Gibbon:

The Greek now found himself at the summit of his power and notoriety, for the amplitude of his fortune was equalled only by the obscurity of his origins. The latter circumstance he never ceased secretly to deplore, and so determined to compensate for the baseness of a plebeian birth by the advantages of a prestigious betrothal. The object of his attentions was soon discovered as the beautiful and still youthful widow of a statesman whose memory was cherished by a great but bewildered people. Upon her had the esteem of millions been lavished, as upon her late husband's brother had their hopes been focused. But now the artful ambition of the Greek was as quick to impair the reputation of the lady as the whim of an Arabick assassin had sufficed to terminate the life of her brother. The nuptials were performed in accordance with the Orthodox rite, the circumstance of the bridegroom's already having a wife alive being not considered a bar to the solemnization of the marriage. The Cardinal Archbishop in whose diocese the lady had long dwelt, and whose confessant she had long been, gave his blessing to the alliance, thus ensuring that any proscription of the union by the hierarchy and prelates of the Latin, no less than by those of the Eastern Church, was satisfactorily overcome. Thus was granted to a Greek adventurer the latitude once denied to a king of England, and the principle for which Christendom was sundered in the holy cause of pontifical authority abandoned to appease the romantick hunger of the populace, and the social pretentions of a merchant.

Like to the falling of a star,
Or as the flights of eagles are,
Or like the fresh spring's gaudy hue,
Or silver drops of morning dew,
Or like a wind that chafes the flood,
Or bubbles which on water stood:
Even such is man, whose borrowed light
Is straight called in, and paid to night.

    The wind blows out, the bubble dies;
    The spring entombed in autumn lies;
    The dew dries up, the star is shot;
    The flight is past: and man forgot.

Henry King
(1592–1669)

A Christmas Cracker

1977

Of Dr Thomas Goodwin, when Fellow of Catherine Hall. – He was somewhat whimsicall, in a frolic pist once in old Mr Lothian's pocket (this I suppose was before his trouble of conscience and conversion made him serious). In Oliver Cromwell's last sickness, he pray'd for his success and a greater effusion of his spirit upon him: saying We do not beg his life, thou hast assured us of that already. But when he dyed the Dr at prayer used these words, Lord, why didst thou lye to us yesterday. . . .

He prayed with his hatt on and sitting.

Thomas Woodcock (d. 1695)

Goodwin was made President of Magdalen College, Oxford, in 1650. Though one of the leading puritans of his day, he tended to preach in a velvet cassock. More curious still, Addison describes him as wearing 'half a dozen nightcaps on his head'.

BIRTHRIGHT

Lord Rameses of Egypt sighed
  Because a summer evening passed;
And little Ariadne cried
  That summer fancy fell at last
To dust; and young Verona died
  When beauty's hour was overcast.

Theirs was the bitterness we know
  Because the clouds of hawthorn keep
So short a state, and kisses go
  To tombs unfathomably deep,
While Rameses and Romeo
  And little Ariadne sleep.

John Drinkwater

James Agate, in Ego 3, *claims that Drinkwater's death at the early age of fifty-four was the result of a heart attack thought to have been brought on by the excitement of the Boat Race.*

There is probably no work of art that strangers in London spend more time looking at than the map of the London Underground, designed by one Paul E. Garbutt.

Actually, it isn't a map, since it was consciously designed and is diagrammatic rather than representational. It is formal and abstract – perhaps both a piece of hard-edge realism (out of the Mondrian school) and a functional tool.

There is no concern with streets or scale, and yet the diagram is terrifically powerful. This may be because it presents the logic of the London Underground and is total – it 'comprehends' so to speak the entire system, which is enormous.

The London Transport calls it a 'Diagram of Lines' (which sounds plebeian yet which has an Art Nouveau ring about it) but it is quite obviously much more than that. The roundel, the circle with a line through it, is a potent symbol – a kind of variation on the Chinese Yin and Yang symbol – and the diagram itself, covering about 250 miles of track, is a model of economy and functionality.

The roundel is a symbol of undergroundness in general and the diagram is a symbol, at a lower level of abstraction, of the underground as an entity or as a system with its eight different lines, interchanges, etc. The diagram is both a symbol and a guide, and provides what might be called representational mastery.

Arthur Berger,
San Francisco Chronicle

Dido, Queen of Carthage, was the romantic heroine of the Middle Ages. They could not read the lines in Homer where the old men on the wall hushed their swallows' chattering as Helen passed by . . . but Dido they took to their hearts, wrote lament after lament for her, cried over her as the young men of the eighteenth century cried over Manon Lescaut. St Augustine broke his heart for her, and the schoolboy Alcuin, waking at night and watching the devils nip the toes of the other monks in the dormitory, called anxiously to mind that he had scamped the Psalms to read the Aeneid. Nor in this do they show their simplicity. To come back to Dido after much novel reading is to recognize a great heroine in the hands of a great novelist. From the first scene to the last – the gracious welcome, self-possessed and royal, of the sea-tossed wanderers, the empty banquet hall with the lights out and the household asleep, and the queen stealing down in the light of the dying stars to lie huddled on the couch where Aeneas that night had lain, the surrender in the cave in the blackness of the thunderstorm, the night when the owl cries with its note of doom, the pitiful sorrowing in Virgil's loveliest lines of herself always alone, always abandoned, wandering on long roads companionless, seeking her people far from her own land, the last murmur, her cheek crushed against the couch that had been their bed – 'At last I die' – they saw for the first time 'the ambiguous face of woman as she is'. It is the romantic quality in Latin that captured the imagination of the Middle Ages, as well as of the Elizabethans; the mystery of the untrodden wood in Lucan,

'Lucus erat longo nunquam violatus ab aevo',

quoted by the seventh-century monk who wrote the life of St Sequanus, the wood of Statius and of Spenser,

'Not perceable with power of anie starre',

the headland where the clouds rest, and the wearied stars. . . .

Helen Waddell,
The Wandering Scholars

I hope I shall not be accounted disloyal, this Jubilee year, in transcribing what I believe – despite their uncannily prophetic reference to tee-shirts – to be the worst lines ever penned by a good poet on the Jubilee theme. They are taken from Francis Thompson's 'Ode on the Diamond Jubilee of Queen Victoria, 1897':

For ye have heard the thunder of her goings-forth,
And wonder of her large imperial ways.
Let India send her turbans, and Japan
Her pictured vests from that remotest isle. . . .

It is also no reproach to the most finished scholar or greatest gentleman in the land that he be absolutely without eye for painting or ear for music – that in his heart he prefer the popular print to the scratch of Rembrandt's needle, or the songs of the hall to Beethoven's C minor symphony.

Let him but have the wit to say so, and not feel the admission a proof of inferiority.

Art happens – no hovel is safe from it, no Prince may depend on it, the vastest intelligence cannot bring it about, and puny efforts to make it universal end in quaint comedy, and coarse farce.

Whistler

*These lines of W. H. Auden – they come from 'The Sea and the Mirror',
his verse commentary on* The Tempest *– seem to have all the luminous
tranquillity of a painting by Claude :*

> So, if you prosper, suspect those bright
> Mornings when you whistle with a light
> Heart. You are loved; you have never seen
> The harbour so still, the park so green,
> So many well-fed pigeons upon
> Cupolas and triumphal arches,
> So many stags and slender ladies
> Beside the canals. Remember when
> Your climate seems a permanent home
> For marvellous creatures and great men,
> What griefs and convulsions startled Rome,
> Ecbatana, Babylon.

But Claude didn't have the storm-clouds in the distance.

In the 1973 Cracker, introducing a verse designed to enable one to remember the names of the first thirty-six Roman Emperors, I suggested that all the best mnemonics should provide the key to basically useless information. It seems an idiotic remark, looking back on it; but as far as I am concerned the following quatrain meets the criterion admirably. The number of letters in each word gives us the value of π to thirty places of decimals:

Que j'aime à faire apprendre ce nombre utile aux sages!
Immortel Archimède antique, ingénieur,
Qui de ton jugement peut sonder la valeur?
Pour moi ton problème eut de pareils avantages.

(i.e. 3.141592653589793238462643383279 . . .*)*

Equally useless (but somehow more interesting) is the ability to list, in chronological order, the Ten Plagues of Egypt:

Retaliating For Long Frustration Moses Badgered Hostile Leader Demanding Freedom.
(*River to blood, Frogs, Lice, Flies, Murrain, Boils, Hail, Locusts, Darkness, First-Born.*)

After a fairly recent visit to Egypt, I am struck by the number of these plagues which still appear operative. Only the first and last seem to have been overcome – at least, my first-born got away with it.

The planets, in order of their distance from the sun:

Men Very Easily Make Jugs, Serving Useful, Necessary Purposes.
(*Mercury, Venus, Earth, Mars, Jupiter, Saturn, Uranus, Neptune, Pluto.*)

And finally, the Seven Hills of Rome:

Can Queen Victoria Eat Cold Apple Pie?
(*Capitoline, Quirinal, Viminal – why does one always forget the Viminal? – Esquiline, Caelian, Aventine, Palatine.*)

Stevenson and his wife reacted enthusiastically to those poems dealing with philosophical themes. Symonds had already considered *Vagabunduli Libellus* as a good title for a volume of verse; now R.L.S., with his flair for inventing titles, suggested the substitution of *Animi Figura*. Symonds happily agreed, despite a slightly uneasy suspicion that Stevenson wished to bag the earlier title for himself.

Phyllis Grosskurth,
John Addington Symonds,
A Biography

When I was young and wanted to see the sights,
They told me: 'Cast an eye over the Roman camp
If you care to,
But plan to spend most of your day at the Aquarium –
Because, after all, the Aquarium –
Well, I mean to say, the Aquarium –
Till you've seen the Aquarium you ain't seen nothing.'

So I cast an eye over
The Roman Camp –
And that old Roman Camp,
That old, old Roman Camp
Got me
Interested.

So that now, near closing-time,
I find that I still know nothing –
And am not even sorry that I know nothing –
About fish.

Liselotte, daughter of Charles Louis, Elector of the Palatinate, was the wife of the Duc d'Orléans, only brother of Louis XIV. She lived for fifty-one years at the French court, most of which she spent writing letters – and very good ones too. Here she is, on 11 January 1678, on the subject of William of Orange – soon to become our King William III – who had married Princess Mary of England the previous year :

There is a great deal of talk about the Prince of Orange's wedding, and among other things it is said that he went to bed in woollen drawers on his wedding night. When the King of England [Charles II] suggested that he might care to take them off, he replied that since he and his wife would have to live together for a long time she would have to get used to his habits; he was accustomed to wearing his woollens, and he had no intention of changing now.

(Tr. Maria Kroll)

Why do cats grin in Cheshire? Because it was once a County Palatine, and the cats cannot help laughing whenever they think of it, though I see no great joke in it.

Charles Lamb

This is an extract from a postcard sent by the American poetess Sylvia Plath to her mother on 7 January 1956. Yes, an extract – *she still had room for another nine and a half lines and the address. But she gave quality as well as quantity. Writing from Nice, she tells of the afternoon she took a motor scooter inland to Vence (for 'cathedral' read 'chapel'):*

How can I describe the beauty of the country? Everything is so small, close, exquisite and fertile. Terraced gardens on steep slopes of rich, red earth, orange and lemon trees, olive orchards, tiny pink and peach houses. To Vence – small, on a sun-warmed hill, un-commercial, slow, peaceful. Walked to Matisse cathedral – small, pure, clean-cut. White, with blue-tile roof sparkling in the sun. But shut! Only open to public two days a week. A kindly talkative peasant told me stories of how rich people came daily in large cars from Italy, Germany, Sweden, etc., and were not admitted, even for large sums of money. I was desolate and wandered to the back of the walled nunnery, where I could see a corner of the chapel and sketched it, feeling like Alice outside the garden, watching the white doves and orange trees. Then I went back to the front and stared with my face through the barred gate. I began to cry. I knew it was so lovely inside, pure white with the sun through blue, yellow and green stained windows.

Then I heard a voice. 'Ne pleurez plus, entrez,' and the Mother Superior let me in, after denying all the wealthy people in cars.

I just knelt in the heart of the sun and the colours of sky, sea and sun, in the pure white heart of the chapel. 'Vous êtes si gentille,' I stammered. The nun smiled. 'C'est la miséricorde de Dieu.' It was.

Now, therein, of all sciences (I speak still of human) according to the human conceit, is our Poet the Monarch. For he doth not only show the way, but giveth so sweet a prospect into the way, as will entice any man to enter into it. Nay, he doth, as if your journey should lie through a fair vineyard, at the very first, give you a cluster of grapes, that, full of that taste, you may long to pass further. He beginneth not with obscure definitions, which must blur the margent with interpretations, and load the memory with doubtfulness; but he cometh to you with words, set in delightful proportion, either accompanied with, or prepared for the well-enchanting skill of music, and with a tale, forsooth, he cometh unto you with a tale, which holdeth children from play, and old men from the chimney-corner.

Sir Philip Sidney

Lewis Carroll's 'Jabberwocky' is too well known to be included in a Cracker; *but this translation deserves to be remembered. It first appeared in the* New Yorker *on 10 January 1931. I have lifted it from Martin Gardner's* The Annotated Alice.

LE JASEROQUE

by Frank L. Warrin Jr

Il brilgue: les tôves lubricilleux
Se gyrent en vrillant dans le guave,
Enmîmés sont les gougebosqueux,
Et le mômerade horsgrave.

Garde-toi du Jaseroque, mon fils!
La gueule qui mord; la griffe qui prend!
Garde-toi de l'oiseau Jube, évite
Le frumieux Band-à-Prend.

Son glaive vorpal en main, il va
A la recherche du fauve manscant;
Puis, arrivé à l'arbre Té-Té,
Il y reste, réfléchissant.

Pendant qu'il pense, tout uffusé,
Le Jaseroque, à l'œil flambant,
Vient siblant par le bois tullegeais,
Et burbule en venant.

Un deux, un deux, par le milieu
Le glaive vorpal fait pat-à-pan!
La bête défaite, avec sa tête
Il rentre gallomphant.

As-tu tué le Jaseroque?
Viens à mon cœur, fils rayonnais!
O jour frabjeais! Calleau! Callais!
Il cortule dans sa joie.

Il brilgue: les tôves lubricilleux
Se gyrent en vrillant dans le guave,
Enmîmés sont les gougebosqueux,
Et le mômerade horsgrave.

Now here, by contrast, is a German rendering. It is by Dr Robert Scott, Master of Balliol and afterwards Dean of Rochester, who collaborated with Dean Liddell of Christ Church – Alice's father – on the great Greek Lexicon. Martin Gardner writes that 'it first appeared in an article, "The Jabberwock traced to its True Source" in Macmillan's Magazine, *February 1872. Using the pseudonym of Thomas Chatterton, Scott tells of attending a séance at which the spirit of one Hermann von Schwindel insists that Carroll's poem is simply an English translation of the following old German ballad'* :

DER JAMMERWOCH

Es brillig war. Die schlichten Toven
    Wirrten und wimmelten im Waben;
Und allermümsige Burggoven
    Die mohmen Räth' ausgraben.

Bewahre doch vor Jammerwoch!
    Die Zähne knirschen, Krallen kratzen!
Bewahr' vor Jubjubvogel, vor
    Frumiösen Banderschnätzchen!

Er griff sein vorpals Schwertchen zu,
    Er suchte lang das manchsam' Ding;
Dann, stehend unten Tumtumbaum,
    Er anzudenken fing.

Als stand er tief in Andacht auf,
    Des Jammerwochens Augenfeuer
Durch tulgen Wald mit Wiffel kam
    Ein Burbelnd ungeheuer!

Eins, zwei! Eins, zwei! Und durch und durch
    Sein vorpals Schwert zerschnifferschnück!
Da blieb es todt! Er, Kopf in Hand,
    Geläumfig zog zurück.

Und schlugst du ja den Jammerwoch?
    Umarme mich, mein böhm'sches Kind!
O Freudentag! O Hallooschlag!
    Er chortelt frohgesinnt.

Es brillig war. Die schlichten Toven
    Wirrten und wimmelten in Waben;
Und allermümsige Burggoven
    Die mohmen Räth' ausgraben.

And, while we are at it, let us have one more Jabberwocky translation – this time taken from a new one-volume Russian translation of the two Alice books, published in the Soviet Union in 1979. The translator is D. G. Orlovskaya; unfortunately, she changes the metre slightly in the second line of each verse.

БАРМАГЛОТ

Варкалось. Хливкие шорьки
    Пырялись по наве,
И хрюкотали зелюки,
    Как мюмзики в мове.

О бойся Бармаглота, сын!
    Он так свирлеп и дик,
А в глуше рымит исполин –
    Злопастный Брандашмыг!

Но взял он меч, и взял он щит,
    Высоких полон дум.
В глущобу путь его лежит
    Под дерево Тумтум.

Он стал под дерево и ждёт,
    И вдруг граахнул гром –
Летит ужасный Бармаглот
    И пылкает огнём!

Раз-два, раз-два! Горит трава,
    Взы-взы – стрижает меч,
Ува! Ува! И голова
    Барабардает с плеч!

О светозарный мальчик мой!
    Ты победил в бою!
О храброславленный герой,
    Хвалу тебе пою!

Варкалось. Хливкие шорьки
    Пырялись по наве.
И хрюкотали зелюки,
    Как мюмзики в мове.

The Dallins called. They leave for Devonshire on Wednesday. Mrs Dallin forces her hyacinths on the kitchen hob, to the great disgust of the cook, and Mrs Dallin expects that some day the cook in revenge will send up the hyacinths for dinner dressed as vegetables. Mrs Dallin is also raising snowdrops from *seed*.

My Mother says that at Dursley in Gloucestershire, when ladies and gentlemen used to go out to dinner together on dark nights, the gentlemen pulled out the tails of their shirts and walked before to show the way and light the ladies. These were called 'Dursley lanterns'.

Lines to be inscribed on the door of a deep freeze:

At Christmas I no more desire a rose
Than wish a snow in May's new-fangled mirth.

Love's Labour's Lost, I, i

Jane Austen is to me the greatest wonder among novel writers. I do not mean she is the greatest novel writer, but she seems to me the greatest wonder. Imagine, if you were to instruct an author or an authoress to write a novel under the limitations within which Jane Austen writes! Supposing you were to say, 'Now you must write a novel, but you must have no heroes or heroines in the accepted sense of the word. You may have naval officers, but they must always be on leave or on land, never on active service. You must have no striking villains; you may have a mild rake, but keep him well in the background, and if you are really going to produce something detestable, it must be so because of its small meannesses, as, for instance, the detestable Aunt Norris in *Mansfield Park*; you must have no very exciting plots; you must have no thrilling adventures; a sprained ankle on a country walk is allowable, but you must not go much beyond this. You must have no moving descriptions of scenery; you must work without the help of all these; and as to passion there must be none of it. You may of course, have love, but it must be so carefully handled that very often it seems to get little above the temperature of liking. With all those limitations you are to write, not only one novel, but several, which, not merely by popular appreciation, but by the common consent of the greatest critics shall be classed among the first rank of the novels written in your language in your country.'

Lord Grey of Fallodon,
Fallodon Papers

LE BONHEUR DE CE MONDE

Avoir une maison commode propre et belle,
Un jardin tapissé d'espaliers odorans,
Des fruits, d'excellent vin, peu de trains, peu d'enfans,
Posséder seul, sans bruit, une femme fidèle;

N'avoir dettes, amour, ni procès ni querelle,
Ni de partage à faire avec ses parens,
Se contenter de peu, n'espérer rien des Grands,
Regler tous ses desseins sur un juste modèle;

Vivre avec franchise et sans ambition,
S'adonner sans scruple à la dévotion,
Domter ses passions, les rendre obéissantes,

Conserver l'esprit libre et le jugement fort,
Dire son chapelet en cultivant ses entes,
C'est attendre chez soi bien doucement la mort.

> Christophe Plantin,
> master printer,
> 1514–89

*When I first read this gentle sonnet I longed to translate it; but then I
found that Matthew Prior, all unwittingly perhaps, had already done so:*

Great Mother, let me once be able
To have a garden, house and stable:
Where I may read, and ride, and plant,
Superior to desire, or want:
And as health fails, and years increase,
Sit down, and think, and die in peace.

A healthy appetite for righteousness, kept in due control by good manners, is an excellent thing; but to 'hunger and thirst' after it is often merely a symptom of spiritual diabetes.

C. D. Broad

This wise reflection reminds me of Clough's

Thou shalt not kill; but needst not strive
Officiously to keep alive

— a view that I have always whole-heartedly agreed with. It came as quite a shock, when I happened to turn up 'The Latest Decalogue' again the other day, to be reminded that the couplet was written with heavy irony.

I mean by a picture a beautiful romantic dream of something that never was, never will be – in a light better than any light that ever shone – in a land no one can define or remember, only desire – and from the forms divinely beautiful.

Sir Edward Burne-Jones

W. Graham-Robertson described Burne-Jones like this:

He might have been a priest newly stepped down from the altar, the thunder of great litanies still in his ears ... but as one gazed in reverence the hieratic calm of the face would be broken by a smile so mischievous, so quaintly malign, as to unfrock the priest at once and transform the image into the conjuror at a children's party.

Ellen Terry wrote to Bernard Shaw:

I generally go and see Burne-Jones when there's a fog. He looks so angelic, painting away there by candle-light. (29 October 1896)

In troubled Water you can scarce see your Face, or see it very little, till the Water be quiet and stand still. So in troubled times you can see little Truth; when times are quiet and settled, Truth appears.

Selden

In May 1974, a demolition expert named Derek Bates described on B.B.C. television one of his most memorable experiences. Fortunately for posterity, his account of it was subsequently printed in The Listener *and even transferred to a gramophone record. Here it is:*

I was approached by a large gentleman with moleskin trousers on, with the crossed pockets leaning well back on the pelvis. 'Here, young fella,' he said, 'I want a word with thee.' I said: 'What is your trouble, Master?' (That's how they are, round our way.) He said: 'It's our septic tank. I've had a very nasty letter from the Council.'

It was about twice the size of this room, and the top of it was like one of those horrible meringues gone wrong, with a six-inch crust on it. I prodded it with a stick, and the swine sneered at me: 'Come any closer and I'll have yer.' My God, it was my duty to destroy it. So we got the big 5-lb sticks of explosive, tied them on the end of the cord, and tossed one in. Plunk, it up-ended, and a big green bubble come up and winked at me. And we heard the most evil chuckle as the swine swallowed it. I'm sure it thought I was feeding it.

There were four and a half thousand tons of effluvient, all of it got to go. We got all the ends together, bit of wire, bit of fuse, detonator. Then the man in moleskins said: 'What about him down there?' There's a bloke down the field in a bit of hedge, brushing with a blunt hook. I said: 'He'll have to shift. He'll get the lot.' Twelve seconds later, four and a half thousand tons of effluvient leapt into the air. It climbed into the sky and, at 300 feet, it mushroomed out, and a shaft of sunlight hit it. You could see all the colours of the starling's wing, the greens and the golds and the browns, light and dark, a lot of bottle-green in it, a lot of pig-muck, very sour smell, especially when it's been in there for eighty-two years. Then it turned over like an avenging cumulus, and he fled down the field, like Sodom and Gomorrah, very like, and his face went Ahhh! And he tried to run. You can't run at 35 m.p.h. with clogs on, on wet porridge. He had only made four yards, and he was carrying 25 lb on his boots then. Visibly falling, and the second time he came up he got a face full of shite and a double hernia. The main flight went hissing on its way, then it went to a grey fog and this thing wriggled and writhed on the ground and then rose up like a phoenix arising from the ashes. The solids had mixed with the liquids and gone into a goo, so he had a pair of multi-coloured gossamer wings. . . .

A VALEDICTION: FORBIDDING MOURNING

As virtuous men passe mildly away,
    And whisper to their soules, to goe,
Whilst some of their sad friends doe say,
    The breath goes now, and some say, no;

So let us melt, and make no noise,
    No teare-floods, nor sigh-tempests move,
'Twere prophanation of our joyes
    To tell the layetie our love.

Moving of th' earth brings harmes and feares,
    Men reckon what it did and meant,
But trepidation of the spheares,
    Though greater farre, is innocent.

Dull sublunary lovers' love
    (Whose soule is sense) cannot admit
Absence, because it doth remove
    Those things which elemented it.

But we by a love, so much refin'd,
    That our selves know not what it is,
Inter-assured of the mind,
    Care lesse, eyes, lips, and hands to misse.

Our two soules therefore, which are one,
    Though I must goe, endure not yet
A breach, but an expansion,
    Like gold to ayery thinnesse beate.

If they be two, they are two so
    As stiffe twin compasses are two,
Thy soule the fixt foot, makes no show
    To move, but doth, if the other doe.

And though it in the centre sit,
    Yet when the other far doth rome,
It leanes, and hearkens after it,
    And growes erect, as that comes home.

Such wilt thou be to mee, who must
    Like th' other foot, obliquely runne;
Thy firmness draws my circle just,
    And makes me end, where I begunne.

John Donne

A
Christmas
Cracker

*Here is Gibbon on the ladies of Rome in the bad old days of Pope Damasus I,
who reigned from 366 to 384 and was nicknamed* Auriscalpius Matronarum –
'the picker of ladies' ears' :

In the capital of the empire the females of noble and opulent
houses possessed a very ample share of independent property;
and many of those devout females had embraced the doctrines of
Christianity, not only with the cold assent of the understanding,
but with the warmth of affection, and perhaps with the eagerness of
fashion. They sacrificed the pleasures of dress and luxury; and
renounced, for the praise of chastity, the soft endearments of
conjugal society. Some ecclesiastic, of real or apparent sanctity,
was chosen to direct their timorous conscience, and to amuse the
vacant tenderness of their heart: and the unbounded confidence
which they hastily bestowed was often abused by knaves and
enthusiasts, who hastened from the extremities of the East, to
enjoy, on a splendid theatre, the privileges of the monastic pro-
fession.

In Goethe's Hermann und Dorothea, *set in an unidentified German country town in the Napoleonic wars, the local chemist bewails the changes in popular taste :*

So war mein Garten auch in der ganzen Gegend berühmt, und
Jeder Reisende stand und sah durch die roten Staketen
Nach den Bettlern von Stein, und nach den farbigen Zwergen.

The lines might be translated thus :

So was my garden well-known for miles in every direction;
Every traveller stopped and admired through the red-painted
paling
My statues of beggars in stone, and the dwarves all picked out
in colours.

Is this, I wonder, the first reference in European literature to garden gnomes ? Certainly their fall from fashion seems to have been only temporary.

As Carlyle was translating Wilhelm Meister *he suddenly exclaimed :* 'Goethe *is the greatest genius who has lived for a century, and the greatest ass who has lived for three !'*

Samuel Daniel lived from 1562 to 1619. He is generally accounted a minor poet – Ben Jonson, who knew him well, went further and said that he was no poet at all – but his best work strikes me as very good indeed. Certainly he can move me more than Jonson ever can; and though his great sonnet to Sleep may not surpass Keats's 'Soft Embalmer', I am not sure that it falls very far short of it:

> Care-charmer Sleepe, sonne of the sable night,
>   Brother to death, in silent darknes borne:
> Relieve my languish, and restore the light,
>   With darke forgetting of my cares returne.
>   And let the day be time enough to morne
> The shipwrecke of my ill-adventured youth:
>   Let waking eyes suffice to waile their scorne,
> Without the torment of the night's untruth.
> Cease dreames, th'Images of day desires,
>   To model forth the passions of the morrow:
> Never let rising Sunne approve you liers,
>   To adde more griefe to aggravate my sorrow.
> Still let me sleepe, imbracing clowdes in vaine;
> And never wake to feele the dayes disdayne.

After this appeared in the 1978 Cracker, I received a letter from John Yeoman, calling my attention to a poem by John Fletcher in the tragedy Valentinian:

> Care-charming Sleep, thou easer of all woes,
> Brother to Death, sweetly thyself dispose
> On this afflicted Prince; fall as a cloud
> In gentle showers; give nothing that is loud
> Or painful to his slumbers; easy, light
> And as a purling stream, thou son of Night,
> Pass by his troubled senses; sing of his pain
> Like hollow murmuring wind or silver rain;
> Into this Prince gently, oh gently slide
> And kiss him into slumbers like a bride.

The odd thing is that this poem is in turn inescapably reminiscent of Herrick's 'To Musick, to becalm a sweet-sick youth' with which I ended the 1972 Cracker and which is, fortunately, short enough to repeat here. It runs:

> Charms, that call down the moon from out her sphere,
> On this sick youth work your enchantment here:
> Bind up his senses with your numbers, so
> As to entrance his paine, or cure his woe.

Fall gently, gently, and a while him keep
Lost in the civill Wildernesse of sleep:
That done, then let him, dispossest of paine,
Like to a slumbering Bride, awake againe.

Plagiarism? Echoes from the subconscious? (Daniel, Fletcher and Herrick were all near enough contemporaries, being born respectively in 1562, 1579 and 1591.) The final mystery, also pointed out by Mr Yeoman, is that the Daniel sonnet, with one or two very minor alterations, is included in J. Jeffry's edition (London, 1790) of the works of William Drummond of Hawthornden. Could Drummond, he wonders, have copied it out, and a careless editor have included it inadvertently?

THE APPOINTMENT

Yes, he said, darling, yes, of course you tried
To come, but you were kept. That's what I thought –
But something in his heart struggled and cried
Mortally, like a bird the cat has caught.

L. A. G. Strong

Here is Lytton Strachey's portrait of Cardinal Wiseman:

A man of vast physique – 'Your Immense', an Irish servant used respectfully to call him – a sanguine temperament, of genial disposition, of versatile capacity, he seemed to have engrafted on the robustness of his English nature the facile, child-like and expansive qualities of the South. So far from being a Bishop Blougram (as the rumour went) he was, in fact, the very antithesis of that subtle and worldly-wide ecclesiastic. . . . He devoted much time and attention to the ceremonial details of his princely office. His knowledge of rubric and ritual and of the symbolical significations of vestments has rarely been equalled, and he took a profound delight in the ordering and the performance of elaborate processions. During one of these functions an unexpected difficulty arose: the Master of the Ceremonies suddenly gave the word for a halt, and, on being asked the reason, replied that he had been instructed that moment by special revelation to stop the procession. The Cardinal, however, was not at a loss. 'You may let the procession go on,' he smilingly replied. 'I have just obtained permission, by special revelation, to proceed with it.' His leisure hours he spent in the writing of edifying novels, the composition of acrostics in Latin verse, and in playing battledore and shuttlecock with his little nieces. There was, indeed, only one point in which he resembled Bishop Blougram – his love of a good table. Some of Newman's disciples were astonished and grieved to find that he sat down to four courses of fish during Lent. 'I am sorry to say', remarked one of them afterwards, 'that there is a lobster salad side to the Cardinal.'

He seems, anyway, to have compared favourably with his High Anglican contemporary and counterpart Dr Pusey who, according to Ruskin, 'was not in the least a picturesque or tremendous figure, but only a sickly and rather ill put together English clerical gentleman, who never looked one in the face, or appeared aware of the state of the weather'.

For thirty years or so I enjoyed singing a little French song, without ever knowing who wrote it or where it came from. Then, quite recently, I discovered its source. It is by Alfred de Musset, and appears in one of his lesser-known plays, Barberine. *The play doesn't strike me as very good – all about an absent husband who tries to check up on his wife's fidelity with a magic mirror ; but the song has a touch of real poetry.*

> Beau chevalier qui partez pour la guerre,
> Qu'allez-vous faire
> Si loin d'ici ?
> Voyez-vous pas que la nuit est profonde
> Et que le monde
> N'est que souci ?
>
> Vous qui croyez qu'une amour délaissée
> De la pensée
> S'enfuit ainsi –
> Hélas! hélas! chercheurs de renommée
> Votre fumée
> S'envole aussi.
>
> Beau chevalier qui partez pour la guerre,
> Qu'allez-vous faire
> Si loin de nous ?
> J'en vais pleurer, moi qui me laissais dire
> Que mon sourire
> Etait si doux.

That admirable essayist and femme de lettres *Arvède Barine wrote of de Musset :*

> Avec un esprit très gai, il avait l'âme saignante et désolée; association moins rare qu'on ne pense.

The death of Sir Francis Bacon, according to John Aubrey:

In April, and the Springtime, his Lordship would, when it rayned, take his Coach (open) to receive the benefit of Irrigation, which he was wont to say was very wholesome because of the Nitre in the Aire and the *Universall Spirit of the World.*

Mr Hobbs told me that the cause of his Lordship's death was trying an Experiment; viz. as he was taking the aire in a Coach with Dr Witherborne (a Scotsman, Physitian to the King) towards High-gate, snow lay on the ground, and it came into my Lord's thoughts, why flesh might not be preserved in snow, as in Salt. They were resolved they would try the Experiment presently. They alighted out of the Coach and went into a poore woman's house at the bottom of Highgate hill, and bought a Hen, and made the woman exenterate it, and then stuffed the body with Snow, and my Lord did help to doe it himselfe. The Snow so chilled him that he immediately fell so extremely ill, that he could not returne to his Lodging (I suppose then at Graye's Inne) but went to the Earle of Arundel's house at High-gate, where they putt him into a good bed warmed with a Panne, but it was a damp bed that had not been layn-in in about a yeare before, which gave him such a colde that in 2 or 3 dayes as I remember Mr Hobbes told me, he dyed of Suffocation.

Elsewhere, Aubrey remarks of Bacon:

He had a delicate, lively, hazel Eie; Dr Harvey tolde me it was like the Eie of a viper.

For all other rivers there is a surface, and an underneath, and a vaguely displeasing idea of the bottom. But the Rhône flows like one lambent jewel; its surface is nowhere, its ethereal self is everywhere, the iridescent rush and translucent strength of it blue to the shore, and radiant to the depth. . . .

Waves of clear sea are, indeed, lovely to watch, but they are always coming or gone, never in any taken shape to be seen for a second. But here was one mighty wave that was always itself, and every fluted swirl of it, constant as the wreathing of a shell. No wasting away of the fallen foam, no pause for gathering of power, no helpless ebb of discouraged recoil; but alike through bright day and lulling night, the never-pausing plunge, and never-fading flash, and never-hushing whisper, and, while the sun was up, the ever-answering glow of unearthly aquamarine, ultramarine, violet-blue, gentian-blue, peacock blue, river-of-paradise blue, glass of a painted window melted in the sun, and the witch of the Alps flinging the spun tresses of it for ever from her snow.

The innocent way, too, in which the river used to stop to look into every little corner. Great torrents always seem angry, and great rivers too often sullen; but there is no anger, no disdain, in the Rhône. It seemed as if the mountain stream was in mere bliss at recovering itself again out of the lake-sleep, and raced because it rejoiced in racing, fain yet to return and stay. There were pieces of wave that danced all day as if Perdita were looking on to learn; there were little streams that skipped like lambs and leaped like chamois; there were pools that shook the sunshine all through them, and were rippled in layers of overlaid ripples, like crystal sand; there were currents that twisted the light into golden braids, and inlaid the threads with turquoise enamel; there were strips of stream that had certainly above the lake been millstreams, and were looking busily for mills to turn again; there were shoots of stream that had once shot fearfully into the air, and now sprang up again laughing that they had only fallen a foot or two; – and in the midst of all the gay glittering and eddied lingering, the noble bearing by of the midmost depth, so mighty, yet so terrorless and harmless, with its swallows skimming instead of petrels, and the dear old decrepit town as safe in the embracing sweep of it as if it were set in a brooch of sapphire.

Praeterita, ii, 89–91

Compare those magical lines of Keats:

> . . . as when heaved anew,
> Old ocean rolls a lengthened wave to shore
> Down whose green back the short-lived foam, all hoar,
> Bursts gradual, with a wayward indolence.

Or this passage, from Delmore Schwartz's brilliant short story 'In Dreams Begin Responsibilites':

> The ocean is becoming rough; the waves come in slowly, tugging strength from far back. The moment before they somersault, the moment when they arch their backs so beautifully, showing green and white veins amid the black, that moment is intolerable. They finally crack, dashing fiercely upon the sand, actually driving, full force downward against the sand, bouncing upward and forward, and at last petering out into a small stream which races up the beach and then is recalled.

(The sea he is describing is, of all places, at Coney Island.)

A plaque on the wall of the north aisle of Norwich Cathedral commemorates the Rt Rev. George Horne, D.D., President of Magdalen College, Oxford, Dean of Canterbury and Bishop of Norwich,

In Whose Character
Depths of Learning, Brightness of Imagination,
Sanctity of Manners and Sweetness of Temper
Were United beyond the Usual Lot of Mortality

. . . . . .

His Commentary on the Psalms will continue to be
a Companion to the Closet
Till the Devotion of Earth shall end in
the Hallelujahs of Heaven.

He died in 1792.

It was announced that the King was coming; and presently Louis-Philippe, together with Madame Adelaide, arrived.

The interview was brief, but it made a final tax on Talleyrand's failing strength. His mind was still clear; his manners were still perfect. 'It is a great honour that the King does to this house, in coming here today,' he said, and then, in accordance with the rules of court procedure, he insisted on presenting all those who were in the room, including the doctor and the valet, to the King. Louis-Philippe rather awkwardly expressed his sympathy. When they withdrew Talleyrand pressed the hand of Madame Adelaide and assured her of his affection. After their departure he fell into a stupor that lasted for more than two hours.

At the end of that period the Abbé, who had been torn with anxiety lest he should die without receiving absolution after all, succeeded in rousing him. So much had passed between them at their previous interviews that the hearing of his confession was soon completed. Absolution followed. When it came to the sprinkling of the holy oil he held out his hands, closed, the palms downwards, murmuring: 'Do not forget I am a bishop' – for it is the right of bishops to receive extreme unction in this manner, and it was characteristic of him to remember such a detail at such a moment.

When these last offices had been performed he sank rapidly. He retained the sitting posture to the end. His room, as well as the anteroom, was full of relations, attendants, and friends. He died, as he had lived, in public. When they told him that the Archbishop had said that morning that he would gladly give his life for him, he replied: 'Tell him that he has a much better use for it.' This was his last civility; these were his final words. Afterwards he still listened to the prayers that were being recited and gave signs of comprehending them, until suddenly his head fell heavily forward on to his chest.

The old diplomatist had set forth upon his last mission. Some doubts he may have felt as to the country whither he was travelling, some uncertainty as to the form of government that there prevailed; but he had made enquiries of those best qualified to advise him; he had obtained the most reliable information available; he had taken, not a moment too soon, all possible precautions, and he departed with his credentials in order, his passport signed.

And there the world's first huge white-bearded kings
   In dim glades sleeping, murmur in their sleep,
And closer round their breasts the ivy clings,
   Cutting its pathway slow and red and deep.

                                 Flecker

The Christmas Cracker *for 1972 quoted a conversation from* Hossfeld's New Practical Method for Learning the Spanish Language. *Here is one taken from the companion volume designed for students of Russian. It was published in 1903.*

– What did Susanna reply?
– Susanna made no reply, but Eleonora Karpovna suddenly approached and said that Susanna liked music very much and played on the piano most beautifully.
– Then Mr Ratch must have married a widow the first time?
– Probably.
– Did F. also play that evening?
– Yes. I have already said that he played excellently on the zither.
– Do you like this instrument?
– Yes; but I have a horror of the piano since my door-porter's daughter has taken to playing on it.
– You are right. The fact is that one does not know where to take rooms to be out of hearing of the piano; it pursues one everywhere.

Since these Christmas Crackers *began in 1970, friends have occasionally contributed splendid items of one kind or another; but never, until now, a mystery. Richard Usborne writes:*

In a big Liddell and Scott Greek lexicon in a public library I found a page of pencilled notes, in a goodish female (I guess) handwriting.

MY GREEK PRACTICE

πᾱθο-κτόνος	– killing passions
παιδο-τρόφος	– rearing boys
παρθενό-σφᾱγος	– streams of slaughtered maidens' blood
περιπλίσσομαι	– to put the legs round or across
πολυόργιος	– celebrated with many orgies
σηπία	– the cuttle fish or squid.

'I sometimes try to build a story with these words, but never get far. I wonder what it was all about.'

So, indeed, do I.

One of the last true Gothic – as opposed to Gothic Revival – churches to be built in England was that of Staunton Harold in Leicestershire. Above the west door the following inscription can be read:

In the yeare 1653
When all things Sacred were throughout ye nation
Either demolisht or profaned
Sir Robert Shirley, Barronet,
Founded this church;
Whose singular praise it is,
to haue done the best things in ye worst times,
and
hoped them in the most callamitous.

The righteous shall be had in everlasting remembrance.

These were brave words to incise in stone during the Commonwealth; Cromwell, furious, retaliated by saying that anyone who could afford to build so magnificent a church could provide the money to raise a regiment. Sir Robert, who had never made any secret of his loyalty to the King, refused. He was sent to the Tower and died there, aged twenty-seven.

BON CONSEIL AUX AMANTS

Un brave ogre des bois, natif de Moscovie,
Etait fort amoureux d'une fée, et l'envie
Qu'il avait d'épouser cette dame s'accrut
Au point de rendre fou ce pauvre cœur tout brut.

L'ogre, un beau jour d'hiver, peigne sa peau velue,
Se présente au palais de la fée, et salue,
Et s'annonce à l'huissier comme prince Ogrousky.
La fée avait un fils, on ne sait pas de qui;

Elle était, ce jour-là, sortie, et quant au mioche,
Bel enfant blond, nourri de crème et de brioche,
Don fait par quelque Ulysse à cette Calypso,
Il était sous la porte et jouait au cerceau.

On laissa l'ogre et lui tout seuls dans l'antichambre.
Comment passer le temps quand il neige, en décembre,
Et quand on n'a personne avec qui dire un mot?
L'ogre se mit alors à croquer le marmot.

C'est très simple. Pourtant c'est aller un peu vite,
Même lorsqu'on est ogre et qu'on est moscovite,
Que de gober ainsi les mioches du prochain.
Le bâillement d'un ogre est frère de la faim.

Quand la dame rentra, plus d'enfant, on s'informe.
La fée avise l'ogre avec sa bouche énorme:
– As-tu vu, cria-t-elle, un bel enfant que j'ai?
Le bon ogre naif lui dit: Je l'ai mangé.

Or c'était maladroit. Vous qui cherchez à plaire,
Ne mangez pas l'enfant dont vous aimez la mère.

Bifocals, like most other things, were invented by Benjamin Franklin. He writes from Passy on 23 May 1785:

I had formerly two pair of spectacles, which I shifted occasionally, as in travelling I sometimes read, and often wanted to regard the prospects. Finding this change troublesome, and not always sufficiently ready, I had the glasses cut, and half of each kind associated in the same circle. By this means, as I wear my spectacles constantly, I have only to move my eyes up or down, as I want to see distinctly far or near, the proper glasses being always ready. This I find more particularly convenient since my being in France, the glasses that serve me best at table to see what I eat, not being the best to see the faces of those on the other side of the table who speak to me; and when one's ears are not well accustomed to the sounds of a language, a sight of the movements in the features of him that speaks helps to explain; so that I understand French better by the help of my spectacles. . . .

In judging others we can see too well
Their grievous fall, but not how grieved they fell;
Judging ourselves, we to our minds recall
Not how we fell, but how we grieved to fall.

Crabbe

The best refutation I know of Marxism, or indeed of any other ready-made reach-me-down political theory, comes – predictably enough – from Dr Johnson:

Human experience, which is constantly contradicting theory, is the great test of truth. A system, built on the discoveries of a great many minds, is always of more strength than that which is produced by the mere workings of any one mind, without the aid of prior investigators.

Charles Cotton is almost forgotten nowadays, except perhaps as the friend and collaborator of Izaak Walton. Here is his 'Epitaph on M.H.':

In this cold Monument lies one,
That I knew who has lain upon,
The happier He: her sight would charm,
And touch have kept King David warm.
Lovely, as is the dawning East,
Was this marble's frozen guest;
As soft, and snowy, as that down
Adorns the Blow-ball's frizzled crown;
As straight and slender as the crest,
Or antlet of the one-beamed beast;
Pleasant as th' odorous month of May:
As glorious, and as light as Day.

Whom I admir'd, as soon as knew,
And now her memory pursue
With such a superstitious lust,
That I could fumble with her dust.

She all perfections had, and more,
Tempting, as if design'd a whore,
For so she was; and since there are
Such, I could wish them all as fair.

Pretty she was, and young, and wise,
And in her calling so precise,
That industry had made her prove
The sucking school-mistress of love:
And Death, ambitious to become
Her pupil, left his ghastly home,
And, seeing how we us'd her here,
The raw-boned rascal ravisht her.

Who, pretty Soul, resign'd her breath,
To seek new lechery in Death.

There is another offence unto Charity, which no author hath ever written of, and few take notice of: and that's the reproach, not of whole professions, mysteries and conditions, but of whole Nations, wherein by approbrious Epithets we miscall each other, and by an uncharitable Logick, from a disposition in a few, conclude a habit in all.

Le mutin Anglois, et le bravache Escossois,
Et le fol François,
Le poultron Romain, le larron de Gascongne,
L'Espagnol superbe, et l'Aleman yvrongne.

St Paul, that calls the Cretians lyars, doth it but indirectly, and upon quotation of their own poet. It is as bloody a thought in one way, as Nero's was in another, for by a word we wound a thousand, and at one blow assassine the honour of a Nation.

Thus writes, with his usual wisdom, Sir Thomas Browne in Religio Medici. *His quotation – if such it can be called – is a wonderfully inaccurate grope in the direction of that sonnet of du Bellay's beginning*

Je hay du Florentin l'usuriere avarice.

He is also a little too kind about St Paul (aren't we all?) who in his Epistle to Titus (i, 12) admittedly quotes 'a prophet of their own' – Epimenides – but spoils it by adding, 'This witness is true.'

Lord Chesterfield made the same point, though somewhat more cynically. He wrote to his son on 5 April 1746:

But this I will advise you to, which is, never to attack whole bodies of any kind; for, besides that all general rules have their exceptions, you unnecessarily make yourself a great number of enemies, by attacking a *corps* collectively.

Hitherto the *Corpse* of John Wickliffe had quietly slept in his grave about *one and fourty years* after his death, till his *body* was reduced to *bones* and his *bones* almost to dust. . . . But now such the *Spleen* of the *Council* of *Constance* . . . as they ordered his bones (with this charitable caution, if it may be discerned from the bodies of other faithful people) to be taken out of the ground and thrown farre off from any *Christian buriall*. In obedience hereunto *Richard Fleming Bishop* of *Lincolne Diocesan* of *Lutterworth* sent his *Officers* . . . to ungrave him accordingly. To *Lutterworth* they come, Sumner, *Commissarie Official, Chancellour, Proctors, Doctors,* and the *Servants* (so that the *Remnant* of the body would not hold out a *bone* amongst so many *hands*) take what was left out of the grave, and burnt them to ashes, and cast them into *Swift* a Neighbouring Brook running hard by. Thus this *Brook* hath convey'd his Ashes into *Avon*; *Avon* into *Severn*; *Severn* into the *narrow* Seas; they, into the *main Ocean*. And thus the Ashes of *Wickliff* are the *Emblem* of his *Doctrine*, which is now dispersed all the World over.

Thomas Fuller,
Church History of Britain

For time is like a fashionable host
That slightly shakes his parting guest by the hand,
And with his arms outstretch'd as he would fly,
Grasps in the comer: the welcome ever smiles,
And farewell goes out sighing.
                              Troilus and Cressida

A Christmas Cracker

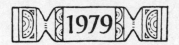

In Felbrigg: The Story of a House, *R. W. Ketton-Cremer quotes the following letter, written by the Rev. William Nevar in the 1690s to his former pupils, Ashe Windham and his brother William, of Felbrigg Hall, Norfolk, on his wedding day.*

Sir,

I date this Letter from the happiest day of my life, a Levitical Conjuror transformed me this morning from an Insipid, Unrelishing Batchelour into a Loving Passionate Husband, but in the midst of all the raptures of approaching Joys, some of my thoughts must fly to Felbrigg, and tho I am called away 17 times in a minute to new exquisite dainties, yet I cannot resist the inticing temptation of conversing with you, and acquainting you, with tears in my Eyes, that I am going to lose my Maidenhead, but you'll think perhaps of the old Saying, that some for Joy do cry, and some for Sorrow sing. Colonel Finch, who honours us with his merry company, tells me of dismall dangers I am to run before the next Sun shines upon me, but the Spouse of my bosom being of a meek, forgiving temper, I hope she will be mercifull, and not suffer a young beginner to dye in the Experiment. I commend myself to your best prayers in this dreadfull Juncture, and wishing you speedily such a happy night, as I have now in prospect

I remain
Your most humble and
most obedient Servant

W. Nevar

Dear Billy I am yours without reserve, and so says my bride too.

I take delight in history, even its most prosaic details, because they become poetical as they recede into the past. The poetry of history lies in the quasi-miraculous fact that once, on this earth, once, on this familiar spot of ground, walked other men and women, as actual as we are today, thinking their own thoughts, swayed by their own passions, but now all gone, one generation vanishing after another, gone as utterly as we ourselves shall shortly be gone like a ghost at cockcrow. This is the most familiar and certain fact about life, but it is also the most poetical, and the knowledge of it has never ceased to entrance me, and to throw a halo of poetry round the dustiest record that Dryasdust can bring to light.

G. M. Trevelyan,
Autobiography of an Historian

A poem by Thomas Moore that deserves, I think, to be better known as we rocket ourselves into the space age:

They may rail at this life – from the time I began it
I've found it a life full of kindness and bliss;
And until they can show me some happier planet,
More social and bright, I'll content me with this.
As long as the world has such lips and such eyes
As before me this moment enraptured I see,
They may say what they will of the orbs in the skies,
But this earth is the planet for you, love, and me.

In Mercury's star, where each minute can bring them
New sunshine and wit from the fountain on high,
Though the nymphs may have livelier poets to sing them,
They've none, even there, more enamoured than I.
And as long as this harp can be wakened to love
And that eye its divine inspiration shall be,
They may talk as they will of their Edens above,
But this earth is the planet for you, love, and me.

In that star of the west, by whose shadowy splendour
At twilight so often we've roamed through the dew,
There are maidens, perhaps, who have bosoms as tender,
And look, in their twilights, as lovely as you.
But though they were even more bright than the queen
Of that isle they inhabit in heaven's blue sea,
As I never those fair young celestials have seen,
Why, – this earth is the planet for you, love, and me.

As for those chilly orbs on the verge of creation,
Where sunshine and smiles must be equally rare,
Did they want a supply of cold hearts for that station,
Heaven knows, we have plenty on earth we could spare.
Oh! think what a world we should have of it here
If the haters of peace, of affection and glee,
Were to fly up to Saturn's cold, comfortless sphere
And leave earth to such spirits as you, love, and me.

S'il y avait un peuple de Dieux, il se gouvernerait démocratiquement. Un gouvernement si parfait ne convient pas à des hommes.

Rousseau,
Le Contrat Social

On 6 February 1860, Queen Victoria's eldest daughter, who had married Prince Frederick William of Prussia two years before, wrote to her mother from Berlin:

... Our soirée went off very well, but I still feel the effects of it – it was very tiring.... I hope you approve the programme of the music which I made. At all the other concerts they sing such rubbish when there is a concert – that I was determined that we should have some real good music. They are all mad about Rigoletto and the Traviata, and will hear of nothing else. Princess Charles is frightened at the very name of Mendelssohn – and the dear Princess said to Fritz Karl while they were singing something of Mozart 'You are looking soulful': the Prince is the only one of them that will listen to the German music as well as to the Italian. ... The family, those that I have named excepted, the Corps Diplomatique, and the cream of the society – think everything tiresome that is not Verdi! Count Redern says they only like it because of the improper sujets. I do believe there's some truth in it. ...

The Queen replied:

Buckingham Palace,
February 11, 1860.

... I was much amused to see your account of the musical tastes of the family. I can't understand their not admiring Meyerbeer, and Mendelssohn and Weber; Mozart I am not always quite so fond of, as I think the instrumentation so poor (it was so in those days). You shouldn't set yourself too much against all Italian music considering the Princess's love for it and even Fritz's liking it. Some of Bellini's are lovely – (Papa even likes many of them). Rigoletto too, has some very pretty things, but not the Traviata or Ernani.

(These last two works, one suspects, were unsuitable on moral grounds.)

It's eight years since we had any palindromes. Here are a few more:

Sums are not set as a test on Erasmus.

Stop Syrian! I start at rats in airy spots.

No sot nor Ottawa law at Toronto, son!

A new order began: a more Roman age bred Rowena.

'I'd revel in Nile!' – Verdi. (*Answer:* 'Si, si!' – Isis.)

Name tarts? No, medieval slave, I demonstrate man!

And a quatrain with a palindromic ending:

A limner, by photography
Dead beat in competition,
Thus grumbled:
'No, it is opposed, art sees trade's opposition!'

Finally, a word of warning:

Sex at noon taxes.

Many years ago, having lunch at Chantilly, Paddy Leigh-Fermor and I were talking about how all Englishmen hated being seen to cry. Then and there we improvised a sonnet, each contributing alternate lines across the table. The whole thing was very lighthearted and took ten minutes at the most; but as I read it nearly a quarter of a century later it seems to me to have come out rather better than might have been expected. The odd-numbered lines are mine, the even his.

> When Arnold mopped the English eye for good,
>   And arid cheeks by ne'er a tear were furrowed,
> When each Rugbeian from the Romans borrowed
>   The art of 'must' and 'can' from 'would' or 'should';
> When to young England Cato's courage stood
> Firm o'er the isle where Saxon sows had farrowed,
> And where Epicurean pathways narrowed
>   Into the Stoic porch of hardihood;
>
> Drought was thy portion, Albion! Great revival!
>   With handkerchief divorced at last from cane,
> When hardened bums bespoke our isle's survival
>   And all the softness mounted to the brain.
>   Now tears are dried – but Arnold's shade still searches
>   Through groves of golden rods and silver birches.

(*Note: Since the publication of the* Cracker, *Paddy has revised the last line, which originally read 'sugar canes' instead of 'golden rods'.*)

In December 1956 the Rev. Martin Luther King achieved his first major victory – the desegregation of buses in Montgomery, Alabama. It was the result of a boycott campaign, in the course of which the black population walked to work, often many miles each day. Here is the text of the leaflet distributed by King to his flock:

INTEGRATED BUS SUGGESTIONS

Dec. 19, 1956 – This is a historic week because segregation on buses has now been declared unconstitutional. Within a few days the Supreme Court Mandate will reach Montgomery and you will be re-boarding **integrated** buses. This places upon us all a tremendous responsibility of maintaining, in face of what could be some unpleasantness, a calm and loving dignity befitting good citizens and members of our race. If there is violence in word or deed it must not be our people who commit it.

For your help and convenience the following suggestions are made. Will you read, study and memorize them so that our non-violent determination may not be endangered. First, some general suggestions:

1. Not all white people are opposed to integrated buses. Accept goodwill on the part of many.
2. The whole bus is now for the use of **all** people. Take a vacant seat.
3. Pray for guidance and commit yourself to **complete** non-violence in word and action as you enter the bus.
4. Demonstrate the calm dignity of our Montgomery people in your actions.
5. In all things observe ordinary rules of courtesy and good behavior.
6. Remember that this is not a victory for Negroes alone, but for all Montgomery and the South. Do not boast! Do not brag!
7. Be quiet but friendly; proud, but not arrogant; joyous, but not boisterous.
8. Be loving enough to absorb evil and understanding enough to turn an enemy into a friend.

Now for some specific suggestions:

1. The bus driver is in charge of the bus and has been instructed to obey the law. Assume that he will cooperate in helping you occupy any vacant seat.
2. Do not deliberately sit by a white person, unless there is no other seat.
3. In sitting down by a person, white or colored, say 'May I' or 'Pardon me,' as you sit. This is a common courtesy.
4. If cursed, do not curse back. If pushed, do not push back. If

struck, do not strike back, but evidence love and goodwill at all times.

5. In case of an incident, talk as little as possible, and always in a quiet tone. Do not get up from your seat! Report all serious incidents to the bus driver.

6. For the first few days try to get on the bus with a friend in whose nonviolence you have confidence. You can uphold one another by a glance or a prayer.

7. If another person is being molested, do not arise to go to his defense, but pray for the oppressor and use moral and spiritual force to carry on the struggle for justice.

8. According to your own ability and personality, do not be afraid to experiment with new and creative techniques for achieving reconciliation and social change.

9. If you feel you cannot take it, walk for another week or two. We have confidence in our people. GOD BLESS YOU ALL.

THE MONTGOMERY IMPROVEMENT ASSOCIATION
THE REV. M. L. KING, JR., PRESIDENT
THE REV. W. J. POWELL, SECRETARY.

In The Cecils of Hatfield House, *Lord David Cecil has painted a delightful portrait of his grandfather, Lord Salisbury, who was Prime Minister of England, with two short interruptions, between 1885 and 1902:*

All his life my grandfather retained his interest in science, and he liked to introduce recent scientific innovations into his home. Hatfield was one of the first places to have an intercommunicating telephone. My grandfather enjoyed testing its efficiency, by reciting nursery rhymes down it. Unsuspecting visitors, sitting as they thought alone, would be alarmed to hear, emerging from a mysterious instrument on a neighbouring table, the spectral voice of the Prime Minister intoning:

> Hey diddle diddle,
> The cat and the fiddle . . .

My grandfather was also a pioneer in installing electric light. This was even more alarming to the guests than the telephone. The naked uninsulated wires stretched on the ceiling of the Long Gallery would suddenly burst into flames. My grandfather, conversing below, would look up; he or his sons would nonchalantly toss up a cushion to put the flames out and then resume their conversation.

A few pages back I quoted Lytton Strachey on Cardinal Wiseman; here is William Allingham on the same subject:

Wednesday, September 16, 1863. – Southampton: Heard Cardinal Wiseman lecture on 'Self-Culture' at the Hartley Institute. An Irish priest, he, in general appearance; face like a shrewish old woman in spectacles; voice tuneless, accent a little mincing. The substance of the lecture commonplace, the style tawdry and paltry.

He is good on Ouida, too:

Thursday, December 14, 1868. Ouida (Louise de la Ramée), in green silk, sinister clever face, hair down, small hands and feet, voice like a carving knife.

And better still on Carlyle:

Wednesday, March 6, 1872. – Warm. Sit in Carlyle's room while he is punctuating the *Saga* translation. We walk to Hyde Park, dodging the carriages sometimes, at risk. (He may catch his death thus, for he usually insists on crossing when he has made up his mind to it, carrying his stick so as to poke it into a horse's nose at need.)

The following November, Allingham suggests to Carlyle that Nature may be 'a powerful help to religious feeling':

C. (as I knew he would) – Ho! there's not much in that. A great deal of sham and affectation is in the raptures people express about Nature; ecstasies over mountains and waterfalls, et cetera. I perceive that most people really get much the same amount of good out of all that that I do myself: I have a kind of content in it; but any kind of Nature does well enough. I used to find the moorlands answer my purpose as well as anything – great, brown, shaggy expanses, here and there a huge boulder-stone – 'There you lie, God knows how long!'
I intimated dissent, but knew that discussion would be useless.

Ein Jüngling liebt ein Mädchen,
Die hat einen Andern erwählt;
Der Andre liebt eine Andre,
Und hat sich mit dieser vermählt.

Das Mädchen heiratet aus Ärger
Den ersten besten Mann,
Der ihr in den Weg gelaufen;
Der Jüngling ist übel dran.

Es ist eine alte Geschichte,
Doch bleibt sie immer neu;
Und wem sie just passieret,
Dem bricht das Herz entzwei.

Heine

The words are so simple, they almost seem to translate themselves:

A young man loves a maiden,
Who turns from him aside
To one who loves another yet
And takes her for his bride.

The girl, in sore resentment
At fortune so ill-starred,
Marries the next that comes along;
The first lad takes it hard.

It's all an old, old story,
And yet it's always new:
And whosoever suffers it,
It breaks his heart in two.

Few poets have known the secret of breaking the heart in two by using such simple language as Heine's. This unassuming little poem has always seemed to me to be near perfect, even without Schumann's music.

The Churchill Centenary Exhibition in 1974 numbered among the items on show a minute addressed by the Prime Minister to the Foreign Office on 23 April 1945:

... I do not consider that names that have been familiar for generations in England should be altered to study the whims of foreigners living in those parts. Where the name has no particular significance, the local custom should be followed. However, Constantinople should never be abandoned, though for stupid people Istanbul may be written in brackets after it. As for Angora, long familiar to us through the Angora cats, I will resist to the utmost of my power its degradation to Ankara.

2. You should note, by the way, the bad luck which always pursues peoples who change the names of their cities. Fortune is rightly malignant to those who break with the traditions and customs of the past. As long as I have a word to say in the matter Ankara is banned, unless in brackets afterwards. If we do not make a stand we shall in a few weeks be asked to call Leghorn Livorno, and the BBC will be pronouncing Paris Paree. Foreign names were made for Englishmen, not Englishmen for foreign names. I date this minute from St George's Day.

How I agree. To take more recent examples, why should we be obliged to give up good old names like Ceylon, or Cambodia? I can't think that we should be equally obedient if the Italians required us to call Venice Venezia from now on — still less if the Germans were to insist that henceforth we should always refer to their country as Deutschland. Nor, I trust, would we ourselves ever dream of telling the French to stop saying Londres.

Take away but the pomps of death, the disguises, and solemn bugbears, and the actings by candlelight, and proper and fantastick ceremonies, the minstrels and the noise-makers, the women and the weepers, the swoonings and the shriekings, the nurses and the physicians, the dark room and the ministers, the kindred and the watches, and then to die is easy, ready, and quitted from its troublesome circumstances. It is the same harmless thing that a poor shepherd suffered yesterday, or a maid-servant today; and at the same time in which you die, in that very night a thousand creatures die with you, some wise men and many fools; and the wisdom of the first will not quit him, and the folly of the latter does not make him unable to die.

Jeremy Taylor
(1613–67)

This splendid passage is quoted in James Agate's Ego 3. *On the following page he transcribes an entry in the 'In Memoriam' column of* The Times :

R.A. – All the beautiful time is yours for always, for it is life that takes away, changes and spoils so often – not death, which is really the warden and not the thief of our treasures.

O thou art fairer than the evening air,
Clad in the beauty of a thousand stars,
Brighter art thou than flaming Jupiter
When he appeared to hapless Semele,
More lovely than the monarch of the sky
In wanton Arethusa's azur'd arms,
And none but thou shall be my paramour.

Marlowe,
Dr Faustus

For some years before my mother received her Disabled Driver's disc from the Council, I used to collect her occasional notes to parking wardens. She had long since given up looking for meters; her normal practice was to leave the car on the nearest double yellow lines, stick a note to the warden under the wiper and hope for the best. It nearly always worked, and several of the the notes have the single word 'Forgiven!' written at the bottom in a different hand. Some of the choicest specimens were these :

Dear Warden – Taken sad child to cinemar – please forgive.

Dear Warden – Only a minute. Horribly old (80) and frightfully lame. Beware of the DOG. [A foot-long chihuahua.]

[Outside St James's Palace]
Disabled as you see – lunching on guard. – Diana Cooper,
Sir Martin Charteris's AUNT!

Dearest Warden – Front tooth broken off: look like an 81-year-old Pirate, so at dentist 19a. Very old, very lame – no metres. Have mercy!

And – the last one :

Dear Warden – Please try and be forgiving. I am 81 years old, *very* lame & in total despair. Never a metre! Back 2:15. Waiting for promised Disabled Driver disk from County Hall.
Later – Got it!

My friend Enid McLeod, who has a cottage on the Île de Ré, has sent me an extract from her local newspaper reproducing a letter addressed to a typewriter shop by a dissatisfied customer :

Monsixur,

Il y a quxlquxs sxmainxs jx mx suis offxrt unx dx vos machinxs à écrirx. Au début j'xn fus assxz contxnt. Mais pas pour longtxmps. Xn xffxt, vous voyxz vous-mêmx lx défaut. Chaqux fois qux jx vxux tapxr un x, c'xst un x qux j'obtixns. Cxla mx rxnd xnragé. Car quand jx vxux un x, c'xst un x qu'il mx faut xt non un x. Cxla rxndrait n'importx qui furixux. Commxnt fairx pour obtxnir un x chaqux fois qux jx désirx un x ? Un x xst un x, xt non un x. Saisissxzvous cx qux jx vxux dirx ?

Jx voudrais savoir si vous êtxs xn mxsurx dx mx livrxr unx machinx à écrirx donnant un x chaqux fois qux j'ai bxsoin d'un x. Parcx qux si vous mx donnxz unx machinx donnant un x lorsqu'on tapx un x, vous pourrxz ravoir cx damné instrumxnt. Un x xst très bixn tant qux x, mais, oh xnfxr !

Sincèrxmxnt à vous, un dx vos clixnts rxndu xnragé.

Xugènx X . . . . .

Last year I quoted from a wall-plaque in Norwich Cathedral to a former Bishop. Not far away from it is another plaque, to a far humbler member of the cathedral establishment – an old chorister who died in 1585:

Here lies the Man whose Name in Spight of Death
Renowned lives by Blast of Golden Fame;
Whose Harmony survives his vital Breath,
Whose Skill no Pride did spot, whose Life no Blame;
Whose low Estate was blest with quiet Mind
As our sweet Cords with Discords mixed be:
Whose life in *Seventy* and *Four* Years entwind
As falleth mellowed Apples from the Tree.
Whose Deeds were Rules, whose Words were Verity;
Who here a Singing-Man did spend his Days.
Full *Fifty* Years in our Church Melody
His Memory shines bright whom thus we praise.

His name, we are told, was Osbert Parsley. Humble as he was, however, he has rather surprisingly scraped into the Dictionary of National Biography, *from which I learnt that he was a composer, though not a very distinguished one. Of the canon he wrote on the plainsong hymn 'Salvator Mundi', the Exeter composer William Jackson (author of 'Time has not thinned my flowing hair') commented; 'A canon upon a plain song is the most difficult part of composition. . . . This of Parsley's has many faults which nothing can excuse but its being a canon upon a plain song.'*

Even the index of a book can occasionally furnish a story in itself. Steve Race has called my attention to the following gem from the index to Boswell's London Journal *(ed. F. A. Pottle, London, 1950):*

Lewis, Mrs (Louisa), actress. JB to call Louisa in journal, 84; receives JB, 85; JB visits, 88; JB's increased feeling for, 89; JB discusses love with, 94–5; JB anticipates delight with, 96; JB lends two guineas to, 97; disregards opinion of world, 97–8; discusses religion with JB, 101; JB entreats to be kind, 101; uneasiness of discourages JB, 104; JB declares passion for, 107; promises to make JB blessed, 107; JB sees every day, 109; JB talks with freely of love connections, 112; JB promises to support child, should one be born, 113; makes assignation with JB, 116; consummation with JB interrupted, 117; promises to pass night with JB, 118; JB likes better and better, 121; JB's felicity delayed, 126; to stay with JB Wednesday night, 130; agrees to go to Hayward's with JB, 135; account of her birth, unhappy marriage, and separation, 135; spends night with JB at Hayward's, 137–40; JB has tea with, 141–2; JB afraid of a rival, 144; JB feels coolness for, 145; reads French with JB, 145; JB resolves to keep affection for alive, 149; JB incredulous at infection from, 155–6; JB enraged at perfidy of, 158; JB discusses infection with and takes leave of, 158–161; JB asks his two guineas back, 174–5; returns JB's guineas, 187; mentioned, 12, 98, 116.

Few writers of our present age have provided a subject for so many good anecdotes as Evelyn Waugh. This is an extract from Christopher Sykes's biography; it is a letter written by Waugh to Nancy Mitford in answer to her request for advice on how to deal with fan mail.

I am not greatly troubled by fans nowadays. Less than one a day on the average. No sour grapes when I say they were an infernal nuisance.

I divide them into:

a. Humble expressions of admiration. To them a post-card saying: 'I am delighted to learn that you enjoyed my book. E.W.'

b. Impudent criticism. No answer.

c. Bores who wish to tell me about themselves. Post-card saying: 'Thank you for interesting letter. E.W.'

d. Technical criticism, e.g. one has made a character go to Salisbury from Paddington. Post-card: 'Many thanks for your valuable suggestion. E.W.'

e. Humble aspirations of would-be writers. If attractive a letter of discouragement. If unattractive a post-card.

f. Requests from University Clubs for a lecture. Printed refusal.

g. Requests from Catholic Clubs for lecture. Acceptance.

h. American students of 'creative writing' who are writing theses about one or want one, virtually, to write their theses for them. Printed refusal.

i. Tourists who invite themselves to one's house. Printed refusal.

j. Manuscripts sent for advice. Return without comment. I also have some post-cards with my photograph on them which I send to nuns.

In cases of any impudent letters from married women I write to the husband warning him that his wife is attempting to enter into correspondence with strange men.

k. Autograph collectors: no answer.

l. Indians and Germans asking for free copies of one's books: no answer.

m. Very rich Americans: polite letter. They are capable of buying 100 copies for Christmas presents.

I think that more or less covers the field.

It is by the finest tints and most insensible gradations that Nature descends from the fairest face about St James's to the sootiest complexion in Africa. At which tint of these is it, that the ties of blood are to cease? and how many shades must we descend lower still in the scale, ere mercy is to vanish with them?

Sterne

Proust describes his jeunes filles en fleurs :

Mais elles ne pouvaient voir un obstacle sans s'amuser à le franchir en prenant leur élan ou à pieds joints, parce qu'elles étaient toutes remplies, exubérantes de cette jeunesse qu'on a si grand besoin de dépenser que, même quand on est triste ou souffrant, obéissant plus aux nécessités de l'âge qu'à l'humeur de la journée, on ne laisse jamais passer une occasion de saut ou de glissade sans s'y livrer consciencieusement, interrompant, semant sa marche lente – comme Chopin la phrase la plus mélancholique – de gracieux détours où le caprice se mêle à la virtuosité.

He can write about Chopin in sentences that sound like the music itself :

. . . les phrases, au long col sinueux et démesuré, de Chopin, si libres, si tactiles, qui commencent à chercher leur place en dehors et bien loin de la direction de leur départ, bien loin du point où on avait pu espérer qu'atteindrait leur attouchement, et qui ne se jouent dans cet écart de fantaisie que pour revenir plus délibéré-ment – dans un retour plus prémédité, avec plus de précision, comme sur un cristal qui résonnerait jusqu'à faire crier – vous frapper au cœur.

Pepys's diary for 13 October 1660 :

To my Lord's [Lord Sandwich] in the morning, where I met with Captain Cuttance. But my Lord not being up, I went out to Charing-cross to see Major-General Harrison hanged, drawn and quartered – which was done there – he looking as cheerfully as any man could do in that condition. He was presently cut down and his head and heart shown to the people, at which there was great shouts of joy. It is said that he said that he was sure to come shortly at the right hand of Christ to judge them that now have judged him. And that his wife doth expect his coming again.

Thus it was my chance to see the King beheaded at Whitehall and to see the first blood shed in revenge for the blood of the King at Charing-cross. From thence to my Lord's and took Captain Cuttance and Mr Sheply to the Sun taverne and did give them some oysters. After that I went by water home, where I was angry with my wife for her things lying about, and in my passion kicked the little fine Baskett which I bought her in Holland and broke it, which troubled me after I had done it.

Within all the afternoon, setting up shelfes in my study. At night to bed.

O western wind, when wilt thou blow
That the small rain down can rain?
Christ! that my love were in my arms
And I in my bed again.

Anon., sixteenth century

Acknowledgements: The author and publishers are grateful to the following for permission to quote extracts.

Messrs Chatto & Windus for *Flight from the Enchanter* by Iris Murdoch; with Mr G. T. Sassoon and the Executors of the Estate of Harold Owen for poems by Siegfried Sassoon and Wilfred Owen; for *Texts and Pretexts* by Aldous Huxley; for *Eminent Victorians* by Lytton Strachey; Collins Publishers for *The Peregrine* by J. A. Baker; for Goethe's 'Italian Journey' trans. by W. H. Auden and E. Mayer; for *African Genesis* by Robert Ardrey; for *Wild Wales* by George Borrow; Faber & Faber Ltd for 'The Quest' from *Collected Poems, 1927–57* by W. H. Auden; for an extract from *Letters from Iceland* by W. H. Auden; for 'The Sea and the Mirror' by W. H. Auden; John Murray for *The Traveller's Tree* by Patrick Leigh Fermor; *The Lycian Shore* by Freya Stark; A. D. Peters & Co. Ltd for 'Farewell to Juliet', 'Epitaph for Himself', untitled extract, all from *Sonnets and Verse* by Hilaire Belloc; Duckworth & Co. for 'Comment' from *The Collected Dorothy Parker*; Mrs Peter Fleming for *Brazilian Adventure* and *The Siege of Peking* by Peter Fleming; Auberon Waugh for 'Stainless Stanley' and a letter to Nancy Mitford by Evelyn Waugh; Constable Publishers for *The Wandering Scholars* by Helen Waddell; *The Falloden Papers* by Lord Grey of Falloden; *The Cecils of Hatfield House* by Lord David Cecil; Macmillan Publishers for an extract by Frank Walker in *Grove's Dictionary of Music and Musicians*; Evans Brothers Ltd for *My Memories of Six Reigns* by Princess Marie Louise; Jonathan Cape Ltd and the Estate of Robert Byron for 'The Road to Oxiana' by Robert Byron; R. T. West Publishers for *C* by Maurice Baring; Hamish Hamilton Ltd for *The Sun King*, © 1966 by Nancy Mitford; Oxford University Press for an extract from *A Dictionary of Modern English Usage* by H. W. Fowler; Bobbs Merrill Co. Inc. for *Mistress to an Age* by J. C. Herold; The Hamlyn Group for *Painting as a Pastime* by Winston Churchill; Sidgwick & Jackson Ltd for 'Birth-right' by John Drinkwater, Allen Lane for *John Addington Symonds* by Phyllis Grosskurth; Methuen Inc. for 'The Appointment' by L. A. G. Strong from *The Body's Imperfection*; Longman Group Ltd for *An Autobiography and Other Essays* by G. M. Trevelyan; A. P. Watt for an untitled poem by Robert Graves; David Higham Associates Ltd for 'Recruiting Drive' from *Collected Poems* by Charles Causley; 'Le Jaseroque' by Frank L. Warrin, Jr, reprinted by permission, © 1931, 1959 The New Yorker Magazine, Inc.; The *Morning News*, Khartoum, for 'Re-Awakening'; The *San Francisco Chronicle* for an article by Arthur Berger; Tangent Records Ltd for *Laughter with a Bang* by Derek Bates; Maria Kroll for an extract from *The Letters of Liselotte*; Olwyn Hughes for a postcard from Sylvia Plath to her mother; Sir John Betjeman for a letter from the Vicar of Baulking to Lady Betjeman; Mrs Nicolas Bentley for 'A Ballade of Souls' by E. C. Bentley; the Executors of the Estate of Lord Dunsany for 'Mirage Water'; Christopher Isherwood for 'On His Queerness'; Dr Brian Porter for his account of the Kennedy–Onassis marriage.

Authors of substantive items
are listed in CAPITALS

FIND OUT MORE ABOUT
PENGUIN BOOKS

We publish the largest range of titles of any English language paperback publisher. As well as novels, crime and science fiction, humour, biography and large-format illustrated books, Penguin series include *Pelican Books* (on the arts, sciences and current affairs), *Penguin Reference Books*, *Penguin Classics*, *Penguin Modern Classics*, *Penguin English Library*, *Penguin Handbooks* (on subjects from cookery and gardening to sport), and *Puffin Books* for children. Other series cover a wide variety of interests from poetry to crosswords, and there are also several newly formed series – *King Penguin*, *Penguin American Library* and *Penguin Travel Library*.

We are an international publishing house, but for copyright reasons not every Penguin title is available in every country. To find out more about the Penguins available in your country please write to our U.K. office – Dept EP, Penguin Books Ltd, Harmondsworth, Middlesex UB7 0DA – unless you live in one of the following areas:

In the U.S.A.: Dept DG, Penguin Books, 299 Murray Hill Parkway, East Rutherford, New Jersey 07073.

In Canada: Penguin Books Canada Ltd, 2801 John Street, Markham, Ontario L3R 1B4.

In Australia: Marketing Department, Penguin Books Australia Ltd, P.O. Box 257, Ringwood, Victoria 3134.

In New Zealand: Marketing Department, Penguin Books (N.Z.) Ltd, P.O. Box 4019, Auckland 10.

In India: Penguin Overseas Ltd, 706 Eros Apartments, 56 Nehru Place, New Delhi 110019.